counting

WITHDRAWN

Cost Accounting
An Essential Guide

**David Russell, Ashok Patel and
Gregory Wilkinson-Riddle**

FINANCIAL TIMES
Prentice Hall

An imprint of **Pearson Education**

Harlow, England · London · New York · Reading, Massachusetts · San Francisco
Toronto · Don Mills, Ontario · Sydney · Tokyo · Singapore · Hong Kong · Seoul
Taipei · Cape Town · Madrid · Mexico City · Amsterdam · Munich · Paris · Milan

To Helen, Luke and Hayley

Pearson Education Limited

Edinburgh Gate
Harlow
Essex CM20 2JE

and Associated Companies throughout the world

Visit us on the World Wide Web at:
www.pearsoneduc.com

_____

First published 2002

© Pearson Education Limited 2002

ISBN 0 273 65167 6

British Library Cataloguing-in-Publication Data
A catalogue record for this book can be obtained from the British Library

Library of Congress Cataloging-in-Publication Data
A catalog record for this book can be obtained from the Library of Congress

10 9 8 7 6 5 4 3 2 1
06 05 04 03 02

Typeset in 10½/13pt Sabon by 60
Printed in Great Britain by Henry Ling Ltd., at the Dorset Press, Dorchester, Dorset

Contents

Preface

The purpose of this textbook is to introduce students to the main principles of cost accounting in a clear and unambiguous way that a novice student will understand and be able to apply to academic problems and real life situations. It is hoped that this will ultimately increase the student's likelihood of success in examinations and other assessed work. It is likely to be of particular benefit to:

- students of professional accounting bodies (ACCA, CIMA, ACA, CIPFA, AAT);
- students completing foundation courses in accounting;
- students studying for undergraduate degree and diploma courses where an introductory costing or similar accounting module must be completed;
- postgraduate students in business and management, where an appreciation of cost accounting principles is required as part of the course;
- other professionals and managers who require a working knowledge of the principles of cost accounting.

The textbook concentrates on the principles of cost accounting, which are fundamental to the understanding of the discipline and will be relevant to students and practitioners alike as they first encounter the subject. It is not intended in this introductory text that specific costing methods such as job costing, batch costing, process costing or joint product costing will be addressed in any depth. Such methods are relevant to a specific business and may not be appropriate for universal study at this level.

The textbook is suitable for integration into a course or as a self-study resource in its own right. It has been written in a consistent standardised format. Each chapter in this book begins with a list of chapter objectives followed by an introduction to the subject matter. The narrative is interspersed with illustrative examples to explain the procedural aspect of the technique, which the reader should find helpful. A key points summary is included at the end of the chapter. The questions for review and self-assessment are designed to reinforce learning and should be attempted. The text is best studied sequentially, however individual chapters may be studied piecemeal if necessary.

Cost accounting is a discipline that arose out of the costing and estimating practices in engineering. Its historical context has been manufacturing, as evidenced by many of the examples used in this text. However, cost accounting is vital to all modern businesses facing increasing competition. Increasingly cost accounting is being successfully implemented in service industries and not-for-profit organisations with significant results.

To our professional colleagues who may find some of the explanations insufficiently pure, we can only emphasise that in our opinion costing is a complex and diverse subject that requires simplification at the outset if it is to be grasped by absolute beginners. Students who made earlier versions of this text a popular choice have vindicated us. There are many excellent texts to progress towards, this one is to ensure that the first step on the ladder is not too high from the ground.

David Russell
Ashok Patel
Greg Wilkinson-Riddle

Chapter 1

What is cost accounting?

Chapter objectives

Having studied this chapter you should be able to:

- explain the meaning and purpose of cost accounting;
- understand how cost accounting arises out of the need to make business decisions;
- differentiate between cost accounting, management accounting and financial accounting;
- appreciate how raw data is transformed into information;
- be familiar with some costing terminology.

Introduction

The purpose of this chapter is to introduce the subject of cost accounting, to explain its relationship to management accounting and to differentiate it from financial accounting.

The survival of any business depends on its ability to settle its debts as they fall due (*liquidity*) and on having products or services that obtain revenues higher than the costs incurred in producing and selling them (*profitability*). The type of accounting which is concerned with recording transactions with outsiders and in determining what the business owns and what is owed to it (*assets*) in comparison to what it owes to the outsiders (*liabilities*) and to the owners of the business (*capital*) at any given time is termed financial accounting. Financial accounting matches the revenues earned in a period against the corresponding costs to measure the profitability of the business as a whole. Thus, financial accounting assists in maintaining liquidity and recording overall profits of the business. Reports based on financial accounting provide useful information to users, the majority of whom are outsiders, who may be interested in the business as a whole. For instance, shareholders and creditors are only concerned with the overall profitability and viability of the business, leaving managers to focus on the profitability of individual product or service lines, using cost and management accounting techniques.

Accounting is multidisciplinary, encompassing financial accounting, cost accounting, management accounting, finance and taxation. The focus of accounting has developed over time from recording financial transactions to comply with legal requirements and for the purpose of a periodic profitability statement (profit and loss account) and position statement of assets, liabilities and capital (balance sheet) to the provision of cost data to assist management in the planning and control of activities and for the purpose of decision making.

Information on the cost incurred in producing and selling individual products or services is not readily available from the financial accounting records. When a business produces different products or services, without such information its managers cannot make sensible decisions about controlling the costs and maximising the profits earned from a particular line of products or services. To obtain this information promptly, a mechanism of recording transactions within the business is required. Cost accounting provides such a mechanism to record the cost of resources used by an individual product/service line, either by identifying the direct connection (*cost allocation*) or by sharing out the common costs on a fair basis (*cost apportionment*).

The role of cost accounting, a discipline arising out of the costing and estimating practices in engineering, is vital to the modern business facing increasing competition. Advances in transportation technology have eroded the geographical barriers to competition, while advances in communication technology have increased consumer awareness about alternative suppliers and their pricing. Increasingly, businesses are facing the challenge of operating in a 'cost continuous' environment with little buffer to absorb poor cost management. Cost accounting assists in cost management by offering various techniques for control and reduction of the different types of costs incurred by a business. It also helps in making the best use of the available resources.

The discipline of management accounting emerged as a natural progression from cost accounting as the information requirements of business managers were better understood and increasingly catered for by accountants. Management accounting is more strategic in nature and encompasses various accounting disciplines such as cost accounting, financial accounting, taxation and financial management as well as behavioural psychology, management science and systems theory. It is beyond the scope of this text to consider management accounting at any depth, however, as management accounting employs cost accounting data there is an inevitable overlap between the two.

What is cost accounting?

Cost accounting is extensively used in a wide variety of businesses, including hospitals, local government, banking, retail and manufacturing. The cost accounting system is the basis of an internal financial information system to assist managers to make business decisions. The types of business decision will vary with the nature of the organisation, but typically these could include:

- whether to provide a new service;
- whether to make or buy a product;
- the extent to which selling prices may be altered;
- whether to manufacture a new type of product;
- whether to increase the levels of service provided.

In an intensely competitive global marketplace, without an effective cost accounting system, it is doubtful whether a business could survive. The ability to determine the costs of products using **product costing** techniques, planning and controlling the enterprise using **budgeting** techniques and making decisions about the future of the organisation using **appraisal** techniques is paramount.

It is important to realise that no two businesses are the same. As a consequence there is no uniform costing system that can be implemented for all businesses. Appropriate cost accounting techniques may be selected from a range of techniques and applied according to circumstances.

There is no law or statute governing the application of costing techniques. Contrast this with financial accounting, where all limited companies are required by law to produce specific prescribed financial statements.

What are the commonly used techniques?

Cost accounting techniques arise because of specific information requirements by management. In some cases this could relate to how much a product costs to manufacture or how much a service costs to deliver. *Product costing/service costing* techniques address this question.

Budgeting techniques assist managers to quantify their future plans in monetary terms and enable comparisons of actual financial performance with planned. Where actual performance deviates from planned this may be recorded and subsequently investigated to ascertain the reasons why this is the case.

Management may also wish to evaluate the way a particular product/service has performed in the past to determine whether the organisation is making best use of the resources available to it, and would also be interested in the future performance of existing and new products or services. In making an assessment as to the viability of a particular product or service, the level of risk associated with it would also have to be assessed and this compared with the possible rewards from the venture, with due regard to management's attitude to differing levels of risk. *Appraisal* techniques assist management to address this matter.

The techniques introduced in subsequent chapters will be introduced under the broad headings of product costing, budgeting and appraisal. They arise primarily out of the requirement to address the information needs of the organisation and provide the data for subsequent analysis by management. These three headings reflect the activities of managers: they plan (budget), measure the results of their plans (record actual product/service costs) and assess the success of those plans (appraisal).

Diagrammatically the cost accounting techniques dealt with in this text are shown in Figure 1.

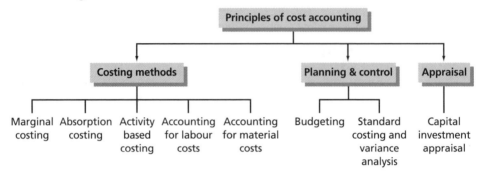

Figure 1 Cost accounting techniques dealt with in this text

The scope of cost accounting

As we have explained, cost accounting techniques arise because of specific information requirements by management. Examples of information required by management and information provided by a typical costing system are shown in Table below.

Specific costing information that could be provided to satisfy the information needs of managers

Information required by management	Costing information provided
Production planning	Cost per unit of production
Methods of production/service delivery	Cost per unit of output
Labour cost control	Labour cost per unit. Cost of downtime and idle time
Material cost control	Material cost per unit. Cost of scrap and wastage
Pricing decisions	Cost per unit of output
Make or buy	Costs at different activity levels
Profit planning	Costs at different activity levels

Summary

- Cost accounting comprises a range of techniques for the purpose of:
  - cost ascertainment,
  - cost control and cost reduction.
- Cost accounting systems and financial accounting systems are different.
  - Cost accounting is in effect for internal use. Financial accounting forms the basis of external reporting and is for stewardship purposes.
  - Cost accounting systems provide information to management for planning, control and decision making.
  - Financial accounting is concerned with types of expenditure for the purpose of an overall profitability statement and statement of assets and liabilities.
- Cost accounting is dealt with in this text within three broad headings of *product costing*, *budgeting* and *appraisal*.
  - They arise primarily out of the need to address the information needs of the organisation.
  - Costing information is not mutually exclusive. It may be used for many purposes.

Questions for review

1 What is the purpose of cost accounting?

2 Discuss the similarities and differences between cost accounting and financial accounting.

3 Discuss the types of information needs that have led to the development of:
   a Product costing techniques
   b Budgeting techniques
   c Appraisal techniques

4 Give *two* examples of where 'cost per unit of output' could satisfy management's information needs.

5 Give *three* examples of business decisions where cost accounting information could prove useful.

Chapter 2

Essential cost accounting terminology

Chapter objectives

Having studied this chapter you should be able to:

- define key cost accounting terms;
- understand the meaning of the term 'overheads';
- appreciate how overheads may be determined;
- be able to classify business expenses using a cost accounting framework;
- demonstrate the importance of aggregating costs on a unit basis.

Introduction

Every discipline utilises a certain amount of terminology or jargon. The purpose of this chapter is to introduce some of the key cost accounting terminology and offer some definitions for the same, with which you will need to be familiar before studying the rest of the text.

You may already be familiar with the typical financial accounting classification used in a profit and loss account, whereby sales revenue (income) is compared with expenses (expenditure) for the same period to determine the profit for the period. Examples of such expenses could be wages and salaries, rent, rates, telephone, stationery, motor expenses, heat, light and purchase of goods for sale if appropriate.

By contrast, cost accounting would classify the same expenses in a different manner. Cost accounting attempts to show in which part of the business expenditure is incurred. For example rent and rates would for the purpose of financial accounting be included in the profit and loss account as an expense being a single total figure. Cost accounting would attempt to redistribute such a cost to the various parts of the business where the expenditure was incurred (e.g. the factory, sales department, head office etc.) and categorise the same using some of the costing terminology discussed in this chapter, thereby providing management with more useful information for planning and controlling the business as well as for the purpose of decision making.

Cost accounting terminology

Direct costs

A crucial method of cost classification is into direct and indirect costs. Direct costs are specific costs that can be identified with a product or service. The three principal categories of direct cost are as follows.

Direct labour cost

The wages paid to employees actually engaged in production or providing the service. For example, in car production, the employees welding the cars together on the production line would be a direct cost. The cost of workers engaged in supervising the activity would not be a direct cost. In banking, a bank clerk serving customers would be a direct labour cost, whereas the cost of a bank manager would not be a direct cost.

Direct materials cost

The cost of buying in the materials from which the finished product is made. This would include all bought in parts and assemblies, but would exclude (say) lubricants for the machinery engaged in the production process.

Direct expenses

Those expenses specifically incurred in the production of a unit of output or the provision of a service. For example, a royalty may have to be paid for each unit of production in a factory. This expense can clearly be traceable to a unit of manufacture.

Indirect costs

Direct costs are specific costs that can be identified with a product or service. It follows that indirect costs are all labour, material and expense costs which cannot be identified with a product or service. Indirect costs are collectively termed overhead. The three principal categories of indirect cost are as follows.

Indirect labour cost

The wages and salaries paid to workers not directly involved in production or service delivery. The cost of workers engaged in supervising such an activity would be an indirect labour cost. Other examples include quality controllers, stores personnel and cleaners.

Indirect materials cost

The costs of all other materials not directly used in production. Lubricants for the machinery engaged in the production process would be an indirect material cost.

Other examples include spare parts for plant and equipment, cleaning materials and stationery.

Indirect expenses

Those expenses not specifically incurred in the production of a unit of output or the delivery of a service. Examples of categories of indirect expenses are:

- **Establishment costs** All the expenses incurred in providing the production or service environment. For example, for manufacturing, this would include the expenses of providing the structure of the factory and the services within it. For healthcare, this would include the expenses of providing the structure of a hospital. Such expenses include rent, rates, insurance and electricity.

- **Selling and distribution costs** All the costs of selling the product or service and delivering it. This includes the salaries and wages of sales personnel and delivery staff, and the cost of transport. Expenses such as rent, rates, insurance and electricity would also be included in so far as they related to the sales and distribution premises.

- **Administration costs** All the costs of directors, managers, administrative staff and similar personnel in the organisation. Again, expenses such as rent, rates, insurance and electricity would also be included in so far as they related to administration.

- **Finance costs** All the costs of borrowed capital. This includes loan interest, any expenses incurred in raising the initial loan and commissions paid to third parties for the same.

Basic classification of costs

Having defined the types of direct and indirect costs, a basic classification of costs statement can be illustrated, as in Figure 2.

The figure includes two important sub-totals in the classification: **prime cost** (direct materials + direct labour) and **cost of production** (prime cost + factory indirect expenses). Some of the terminology used in the statement appears specifically to relate to manufacturing organisations. This is a consequence of cost accounting arising out of the costing and estimating practices in engineering. Statements of this type were originally derived to satisfy the needs of manufacturing organisations. Today service industries are more prominent in the economy and such a statement is also appropriate for this sector. However, some of the descriptions used above may not be as applicable to a service organisation. The descriptions may be modified as appropriate as cost accounting is not required to comply with statutory legal presentation requirements in the

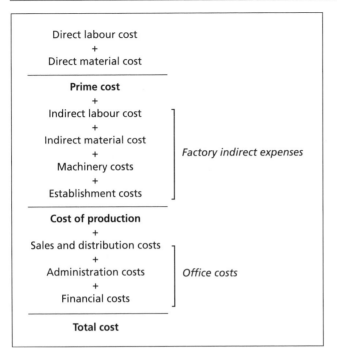

Figure 2 The most commonly used classification of costs for cost accounting purposes

same way as financial accounting. For example, 'sales and distribution costs' may be more appropriately retitled 'external relations and transport costs'.

Further cost accounting terminology

Cost centre

It is necessary to divide a large business into smaller logical parts to facilitate the charging of costs to individual units of output. A cost centre, usually an intermediate stage where expenditure may be gathered for later distribution, is a logical place to assemble costs for a particular organisation. A cost centre could, for example, be a location, a person, an item of equipment or a group of equipment, an inspection department or even sales representatives. Cost centres have the added advantage of clearly identifying individuals, machinery etc., thereby facilitating the relating of costs to individual responsibility.

Cost unit

A cost unit is a unit of output for an organisation. This may be a tonne of coal from a coal mine, or a book loaned from a library. Once cost centres and cost units are established for an organisation, it is possible to charge costs from cost centres to cost units to determine the cost per unit of output.

Conversion cost

This is a term to refer to the costs of converting purchased materials into finished goods.

Added value

The value of a manufactured product, or service delivered, should be greater than the cost of the constituent bought in materials and services. Added value is an important notion that seeks to draw attention to the efficacy of the organisation, by focusing on the activities of the organisation rather than the costs of bought in materials and services, which an organisation can do little about.

An introduction to overhead

Overhead refers to all costs except direct labour, direct materials and direct expenses. Direct costs, by their nature and definition are easily associated with cost units. However, overheads (indirect costs, machinery costs, establishment costs, selling and distribution, administration and financial costs) may be considerable and by their very nature are not so readily identifiable to cost units. For example, it is difficult to determine the appropriate amount of loan interest to charge to a single cost unit, particularly if some cost units take longer than others to complete. See Figure 3.

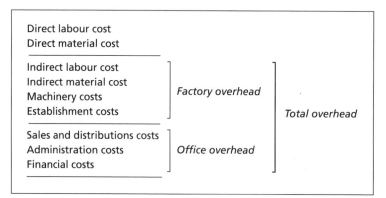

Figure 3 Categories of overhead form a basic classification of costs for cost accounting purposes

Cost allocation

Cost allocation may apply equally to direct costs and overhead. Where a cost may be clearly identified with a cost centre it may be allocated without division or splitting. For example, electricity could be separately metered to a cost centre where the cost centre is (say) the inspection department. In this instance the entire charge for the metered supply may be allocated to this cost centre without further computation. (The allocation for this would take place via the costing system.)

Cost apportionment

Some just and equitable method must be determined to share out very significant costs which cannot be easily allocated to cost centres or cost units. Cost apportionment is an attempt to share a cost between two or more cost centres on a just and equitable basis with regard to the benefit received. The emphasis here is upon fairness in sharing the common cost as it is acknowledged that precisely determining the benefit received would prove very difficult in many cases. For example, office rent could be apportioned on the basis of floor area used by a cost centre. The choice of basis for apportionment is paramount and can prove to be somewhat subjective in some cases.

Overhead recovery

After overhead has been allocated and apportioned to cost centres, it may be charged to cost units using a technique referred to as overhead recovery. Overhead may be recovered using absorption costing or activity based costing techniques (which are dealt with in Chapters 6 and 7 respectively).

Essentially the process involves the recovery of overhead using a predetermined recovery rate based upon the dominant activities involved in the manufacturing process or the service delivery. This could be the number of labour hours, the number of machine hours or the number of inspections carried out.

Determination of total cost

It is appropriate to illustrate the terminology used in this chapter (classification of costs, cost centres, cost units, cost allocation, cost apportionment and overhead recovery) as part of a single diagram (Figure 4), to demonstrate the build-up of total cost.

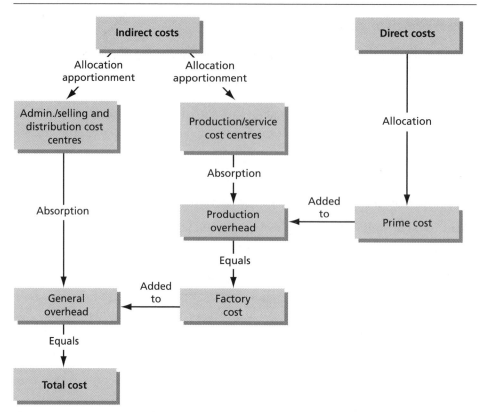

Figure 4 Determination of total cost

Summary

- Cost accounting terminology seeks to differentiate between two fundamental types of cost:
  - direct cost,
  - overhead.

- Cost centres and cost units are derived from the need to be able to charge direct costs and overheads to each unit of output or service delivery, in an attempt to identify the viability of the operation.
  - This may be referred to as value added.

- Overhead refers to all costs except direct costs. Overheads are charged to cost units via:
  - cost allocation,
  - cost apportionment,
  - overhead recovery (absorption or activity based).

Questions for review

1 What is a direct cost and what differentiates it from an indirect cost?

2 Define a cost centre and give *three* examples.

3 What is the difference between a cost centre and a cost unit?

4 Describe
   a Cost allocation
   b Cost apportionment

5 Give an example of a cost unit for a manufacturing organisation.

6 Give an example of a cost unit for a service organisation.

7 Give an example of a cost which is not readily identifiable to a cost unit.

8 What does overhead recovery seek to achieve?

9 What are the *two* principal methods of overhead recovery?

10 What is prime cost?

Self-assessment questions

(*Denotes that a suggested solution may be found at the end of this book.)

1* Classification and categories of cost

The data below relates to the accounts on Univat Ltd, a company engaged in the manufacture of a single product, missiles.

	£
Factory wages, 65% of which are paid to production line staff	40,000
Rent and rates 74% of which is for the factory area	12,000
Sales and admin. offices are of equal size	
Material purchases, 85% of which are for missiles	75,000
Material purchases for other factory materials are 10%	
Material purchases for office cleaning are 5%	
Factory machine depreciation	29,000
Office wages, 50% sales, 50% admin.	18,000
Telephone and postage, 15% factory, 85% sales	15,000
Salespeople's motor expenses	9,000
Delivery costs	15,000
Advertising costs	17,000
Total cost	230,000

a Determine the prime cost of the missiles.
b Determine the cost of production of the missiles.
c What is the total cost of the missiles?
d Determine the factory overhead.
e What is the total overhead?

2* Cost accounting classification
Determine the most appropriate cost accounting classification of cost for the following expenses of a business manufacturing white electrical goods.

a Electric cooker element
b Oven doors
c Wages of the stores person issuing parts to production
d Accountant's salary
e Wages of production workers assembling driers
f Electric motors used in the manufacture of driers
g Welding machines used to assemble the cookers
h Factory telephones
i Repairs to the office block
j Motor expenses for sales staff
k Motor expenses for the sales manager
l Fuel for delivery vehicles
m Foreman's wages
n Interest payments on loans
o Electricity costs for the computer equipment used in both the accounts and sales departments
p Cost of the computer used in both departments
q Oils used in the factory for lubrication of the production line
r Fork-lift truck hire costs
s Wages of the fork-lift truck drivers (located in the stores area)
t Steel used to make the appliances

Chapter 3

Cost behaviour

Chapter objectives

Having studied this chapter you should be able to:

- understand the importance of cost behaviour;
- define a fixed cost;
- define a variable cost;
- be able to demonstrate how cost characteristics may be determined using the high/low method, scattergraph and least squares regression;
- be able to predict future costs based upon historical data;
- understand the difficulties of cost prediction;
- appreciate the difference in approach to cost behaviour analysis used by the accounting model and the economists' model.

Introduction

The purpose of this chapter is to provide some understanding of the different types of cost and the distinct ways they behave under specified conditions. It is important at this stage to consider the behaviour of costs (i.e. what causes certain costs to increase and decrease for a business) in order to:

- determine what costs should have been for an accounting period;
- estimate costs for a future period.

An appreciation of how costs may vary at differing levels of activity within the organisation, as a consequence of differing levels of volume or activity (where volume relates to the production of units or service delivered) is paramount for planning, control and decision making. Familiarity with cost behaviour is therefore necessary prior to studying Chapters 6 to 12 where volume or level of activity has a significant impact on the costing technique under consideration.

What is cost behaviour?

Cost behaviour is the study of the way costs fluctuate and the rationale for such variation. There are two major influences on costs: volume (or activity) and time. It is these two factors that provide the important classification of costs into the following categories:

- variable cost
- fixed cost
- semi-variable cost
- step costs.

An understanding of the different categories of cost is important in the study of cost accounting, and an understanding of the fundamental difference between variable and fixed costs is essential for the application of many aspects of cost accounting.

Variable cost

A variable cost is a cost that varies in direct proportion to some measure of output or activity. For example, the total raw materials cost to manufacture cars would increase according to the number of cars manufactured. Therefore there is a linear relationship between cost and output (or activity), unit variable costs remaining constant. Variable costs usually comprise the following:

- direct labour cost
- direct material cost
- variable overhead.

Figure 5 illustrates how a variable cost would appear on a graph.

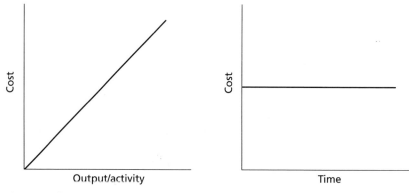

Figure 5 Illustration of a variable cost

Fixed cost

A fixed cost is frequently described as a period cost. Fixed costs vary with time rather than output or activity and will within certain limits remain the same irrespective of the level of output or activity. Examples of fixed costs are:

- rent
- depreciation
- rates
- staff salaries.

For each of the above, costs increase in direct proportion to time rather than output. For example, rent would be paid per month, quarter or per annum and would not increase whether (say) one or 20 cars are manufactured, or one or 20 customers were served during the period. Therefore there is a linear relationship between cost and time, not output (or activity). Unit fixed costs, however, will of course decline as output (or activity) expands, since the total fixed cost remains constant.

Figure 6 illustrates how a fixed cost would appear on a graph

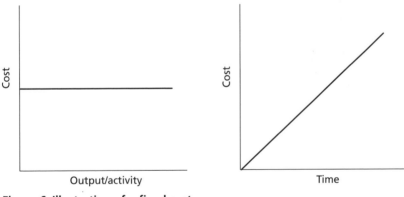

Figure 6 Illustration of a fixed cost

Semi-variable (semi-fixed) cost

In practice few costs are entirely variable or purely fixed. Semi-variable costs (sometimes referred to as semi-fixed costs) consist of both a fixed and variable component. Such costs are affected by both time and output (or activity). An example of a semi-variable cost would be a telephone charge, which frequently contains a line rental component, which has to be paid irrespective of the number of calls made in the period, and a cost per minute for call charges. Other examples of semi-variable costs include:

- electricity costs
- water costs
- gas costs
- maintenance costs.

Figure 7 illustrates how a semi-variable cost would appear on a graph.

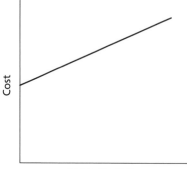

Figure 7 Illustration of a semi-variable cost

Step (fixed) costs

Step costs are fixed over a certain range of output (or activity), but increase in a discrete amount when output (or activity) rises above a crucial range. For example, the salary costs paid to supervisors would remain the same irrespective of other factors, until (say) an additional shift is introduced and more supervisors are recruited. Step costs will increase by a constant amount at a variety of activity levels. Figure 8 illustrates how step costs would appear on a graph.

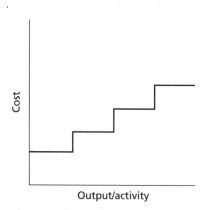

Figure 8 Illustration of a step (fixed) cost

Distinguishing between different cost classifications

As we have discussed, the various types of costs are likely to *behave* in a different manner from each other (i.e. the way in which they increase or decrease under different conditions).

When studying cost behaviour, the cost accountant is only concerned with the *relevant range of activity*. This is the range of output or activity where:

- the organisation normally operates (e.g. 12,000 cars produced per annum or 120,000 customers served per annum);
- the cost estimates will apply.

Within the *relevant range of activity* most items of cost settle into a basic pattern of behaviour of:

- fixed
- variable
- semi-variable.

In this range, only a limited span of output or activity is being considered, as opposed to the whole spectrum of activity or output from zero to infinity. If the relevant range changes significantly, it may be necessary to review cost estimates.

The focus of the cost accountant is therefore quite narrow compared with an economist, who would take a more macro view and would be interested in costs at all output or activity levels from zero to infinity.

It is important to be able to distinguish between the different cost classifications of fixed, variable and semi-variable for the purposes of planning, control and decision making. Typically, the cost accountant may be presented with historical data relating to total cost for a variety of activity levels (albeit within the relevant range of activity) and would be required to decipher the fixed and variable cost element of the same.

There are a number of techniques used for this purpose, three common ones being:

- high/low method
- scattergraph
- least squares regression analysis.

High/low method

This is an uncomplicated technique that utilises the highest and lowest observations from a set of data to determine the fixed and variable cost element. The change in cost at different output or activity levels will be a variable cost, as fixed costs do not change with output or activity. Once the variable cost is established, the fixed cost may be determined as it is the constant element of the cost.

EXAMPLE

	Output/Activity	Total cost (£)
	15	180
	20	230
	17	190
	18	208
	19	220
	11	140
High	20	230
Low	11	140
Change	9	90

The change in cost per unit of output/activity can be determined as follows:

$$\textbf{Variable cost} = \frac{\text{Change in cost}}{\text{Change in output/activity}} = \frac{90}{9} = \textbf{£10/unit}$$

The fixed cost element of the total cost may now also be determined.
   At an output of 20 units where the cost is £230:

	£
Variable cost (20 × £10)	200
Total cost	230
Therefore, **fixed cost**	30

The fixed and variable cost elements may also be determined using simultaneous equations where the equation for total cost is of the type

$$y = a + b(x)$$

where
   y = total cost
   a = fixed cost
   b = variable cost
   x = no. of units produced (or some other measure for activity)

Using the data from the example above:

$$y = a + b(x)$$
$$230 = a + b(20)$$
$$\underline{140 = a + b(11)}$$
$$90 = b(9)$$
$$\frac{90}{9} = b$$

Therefore, b (variable cost) = £10
Substituting b into equation above

$$y = a + b(x)$$
$$230 = a + 10(20)$$
$$230 = a + 200$$

Therefore, a (fixed cost) = £30

The high/low method is advantageous in that it is easy to use, however it does ignore all of the other observations other than the highest and lowest, which may be extremes and unrepresentative of the data as a whole. This could compromise its precision.

Scattergraph

The scattergraph overcomes the criticism of the high/low method by taking into account a greater quantity of data. It is a simple and straightforward technique that requires the drawing of a graph for all of the observations of the data and adding a line of best fit.

The intercept of the line to the y-axis determines the fixed cost. The gradient of the same provides the variable cost per unit.

EXAMPLE

The same data as used in the example above could be plotted onto a graph, as shown in Figure 9(a). A line of best fit may now be added (Figure 9(b)).

The intercept of the line to the y-axis that determines the fixed cost is adjudged to be **£20**. The gradient of the same provides the variable cost per unit and is as follows:

Cost at 10 units is adjudged (from the graph) to be £125

Cost at 20 units is (from the graph) £230

The variable cost is

$$\frac{230 - 125}{20 - 10} = £10.50/unit$$

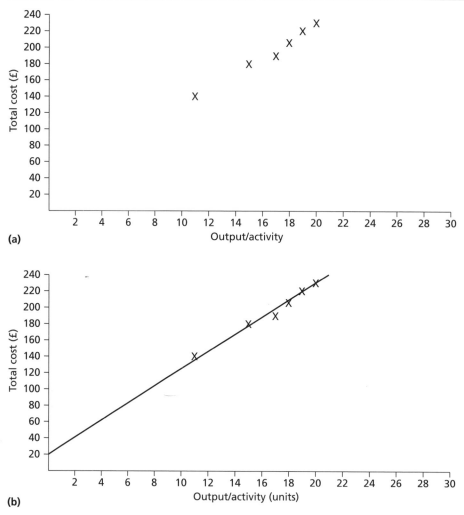

Figure 9 Illustration of a scattergraph

This method is still rather arbitrary as it relies on judgement for the line of best fit, which may be problematic if there is no clear pattern to the data. Again, this could compromise the accuracy.

Least squares regression analysis

Least squares regression is a more comprehensive statistical method that minimises the sum of the squares of the differences between the line and the observations to determine a linear total cost function of the type $y = a + b(x)$ (discussed above). Least squares regression uses two equations to determine *a* and *b*:

$$b = \frac{n\Sigma xy - \Sigma x \Sigma y}{n\Sigma x^2 - [\Sigma x]^2}$$

$$a = \frac{\Sigma y}{n} - b\left[\frac{\Sigma x}{n}\right]$$

where

y = total cost
a = fixed cost
b = variable cost
x = no. of units produced (or some other measure for activity)
n = the number of observations of data
Σ = the sum of

EXAMPLE

The same data as above would be used as follows:

	Output/activity (x)	Total cost (£) (y)	(x^2)	(xy)
	15	180	225	2700
	20	230	400	4600
	17	190	289	3230
	18	208	324	3744
	19	220	361	4180
	11	140	121	1540
$\Sigma =$	100	1,168	1,720	19,994

$n = 6$

These values may now be substituted into the two equations above to determine *a* and *b*:

$$b = \frac{(6 \times 19,994) - (100 \times 1168)}{(6 \times 1720) - 100^2}$$

$$= \frac{119,964 - 116,800}{10,320 - 10,000}$$

$$= \frac{3164}{320}$$

$b = 9.8875$ = variable cost/unit

$$a = \frac{1168}{6} - 9.8875 \left[\frac{100}{6} \right]$$

$$= 194.666 - 164.7916$$

$a = 29.8744 =$ fixed cost

Therefore, the linear total cost function of the type $y = a + b(x)$ is

$$y = 29.8744 + 9.8875(x)$$

where $x =$ no. of units.

Regression analysis is a more precise (and time consuming) method as it takes into account all the observations. The accuracy of regression analysis can be measured by a coefficient of determination (r^2), a discussion of which is outside the scope of this text.

Conditions suitable for the use of regression analysis are that

- a linear cost function should be assumed;
- there should be a high degree of correlation between output (activity) and cost;
- there should be a wide spread of activity levels.

Cost prediction

Once cost classifications are determined, it is possible to predict costs based upon historical data. This may be beneficial in order to:

- determine what costs should have been for an accounting period
- to estimate costs for a future period.

EXAMPLE

Period	Output/activity (x)	Total cost (£) (y)
1	65	700
2	80	850
3	90	950
4	85	900
5	76	810

What costs should be expected in period 6 if output is 70 units?

Solution

High/low method

High	90	950
Low	65	700
Change	25	250

The change in cost per unit of output/activity can be determined as follows:

$$\text{Variable cost} = \frac{\text{Change in cost}}{\text{Change in output/activity}} = \frac{250}{25} = £10/\text{unit}$$

The fixed cost element of the total cost may now be determined.
  At an output of 90 units where the cost is £950:

	£
	£
Variable cost (90 × £10)	900
Total cost	950
Therefore, **fixed cost**	50

The fixed and variable cost elements may also be determined using simultaneous equations (as above).
  Using the data given:

$$y\ \ = a + b(x)$$
$$950 = a + b(90)$$
$$700 = a + b(65)$$
$$\overline{250 = \quad\ b(25)}$$
$$\frac{250}{25} = \quad b$$

Therefore, b **(variable cost)** = £10
Substituting b into the equation above:

$$y\ \ = a + b\ \ (x)$$
$$950 = a + 10\ \ (90)$$
$$950 = a + 900$$

Therefore, a **(fixed cost)** = £50

Scattergraph

Here the data could be plotted onto a graph as shown in Figure 10(a) and a line of best fit added, Figure 10(b).
  The intercept of the line to the y-axis that determines the fixed cost is adjudged to be **£40**. The gradient of the same provides the variable cost per unit and is

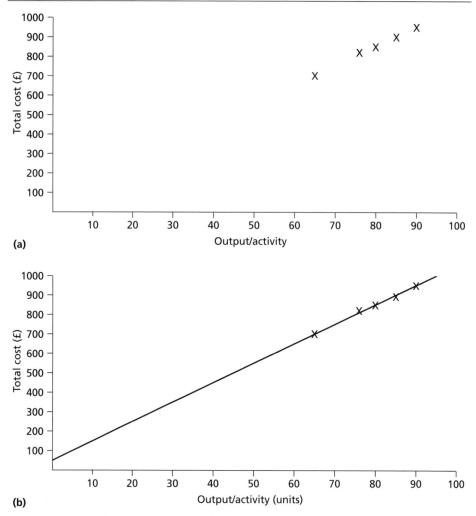

(a)

(b)

Figure 10 Illustration of a scattergraph

as follows:

Cost at 70 units is adjudged (from the graph) to be £750

Cost at 80 units is (from the graph) £850

The variable cost is:

$$\frac{850 - 750}{80 - 70} = £10/\text{unit}$$

As we have explained, this method is rather arbitrary as it relies on judgement for the line of best fit, which may be problematic if there is no clear pattern to the data. The results obtained here for the fixed costs are different from those obtained under both the high/low method and the least squares regression analysis method (see below).

Least squares regression

The data given would be used as follows:

Output/activity (x)	Total cost (£) (y)	(x^2)	(xy)
65	700	4225	45,500
80	850	6400	68,000
90	950	8100	85,500
85	900	7225	76,500
76	810	5776	61,560
$\Sigma =$ 396	4,210	31,726	337,060

$n = 5$

These values may now be substituted into the least squares regression equations to determine a and b:

$$b = \frac{n\Sigma xy - \Sigma x \Sigma y}{n\Sigma x^2 - [\Sigma x]^2}$$

$$a = \frac{\Sigma y}{n} - b\left[\frac{\Sigma x}{n}\right]$$

$$b = \frac{(5 \times 337,060) - (396 \times 4210)}{(5 \times 31,726) - 396^2} = \frac{1,685,300 - 1,667,160}{158,630 - 156,816} = \frac{18,140}{1814}$$

$b = 10$ (variable cost/unit)

$$a = \frac{4210}{5} - 10\left[\frac{396}{5}\right] = 842 - 792$$

$a = 50$ (fixed cost)

Therefore, the linear total cost function of the type $y = a + b(x)$ is

$y = 50 + 10(x)$

where $x = $ no. of units.

Cost prediction solution

Therefore, costs in period 6 for 70 units:

	£
Variable cost (70 × £10)	700
Fixed cost	50
Total cost for period 6	**750**

The difficulties of cost prediction

It must be borne in mind that past costs may only be used as a guide to future costs where conditions have remained stable.

In making any forecast of costs for the purpose of planning and decision making, the analysis of past costs into fixed and variable components is likely to prove invaluable. However, care should be exercised when relying on this data to estimate future costs. The drawbacks of the high/low method, scatter-graph and regression analysis have already been mentioned, particularly with the possibility in some instances of variations in fixed and variable costs depending on the method chosen.

Moreover, past costs will only provide a useful guide to future costs if conditions remain stable.

There are many other factors, which may influence costs:

- the introduction of new technology;
- changes in working practices;
- the market in which the organisation operates may be dynamic and changing;
- volatile exchange rates, where the organisation relies on imported raw materials, good or services;
- changes in taxation rates;
- the introduction of a new product or service.

In such circumstances past costs cannot be relied upon. Reliance may have to be placed upon management's judgement or best estimate for cost prediction.

Cost behaviour analysis: the accounting model vs. the economists' model

In practice it would appear unlikely that all costs would settle into a basic pattern of behaviour of fixed, variable and semi-variable components.

Consider the situation of a firm with a variable cost per unit of £5.50 for a particular type of raw material. If the company were to increase the order for this material, from (say) 20 units to 2000 units per period, a larger discount could be offered by the supplier as an incentive. The variable cost per unit may then reduce to (say) £5.10 per unit. The linear total cost function would be shown as a curved (convex) line on a graph and would be described as curvilinear (each extra unit of purchase causes a less than proportionate increase in cost). Economists refer to this as *economy of scale*.

The accounting model assumes variable costs are linear (i.e. a straight line on a graph) whereas the economists' model assumes they are curvilinear. Figures 11 and 12 illustrate this.

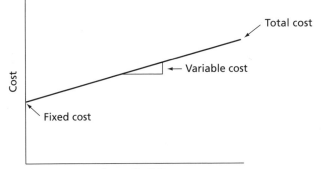

Figure 11 Illustration of a linear total cost function

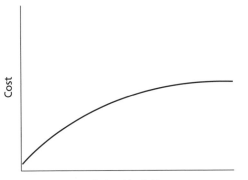

Figure 12 Illustration of a curvilinear cost function

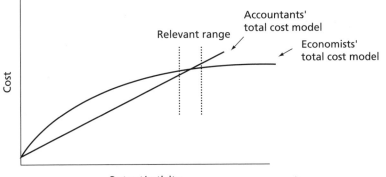

Figure 13 The linear accounting model overlaid onto the economists' model to illustrate the relevant range of output

The accounting model and the economic theory model appear to conflict. However they are broadly compatible within the *relevant range* of output (or activity). This is the range where the organisation normally operates (in our example approximately 20 units per period). Within this range, price and efficiency levels are held constant by management and the linear relationships are likely to hold good. If, however, an organisation operates outside the *relevant range*, it may be necessary to redetermine the cost estimate for the variable cost per unit.

The compatibility of the accounting model and economists' model is illustrated in Figure 13.

Summary

- Within the *relevant range of activity* most items of cost settle into a basic pattern of behaviour of:
  - fixed,
  - variable,
  - semi-variable.

- It is important to be able to distinguish between different cost classifications for the purpose of:
  - Planning.
  - Control.
  - Decision making.

- A variable cost is a cost that varies in direct proportion to some measure of activity or output.
  - There is a linear relationship between variable cost and activity or output.

- Fixed costs remain the same irrespective of the level of activity or output. Fixed costs vary with time.
  - There is a linear relationship between fixed cost and time.

- Cost characteristics may be determined using:
  - high/low method,
  - scattergraph,
  - least squares regression analysis.

- Once fixed and variable costs have been determined from historical data, forecast costs for different output or activity levels may be determined.
  - The use of judgement is important in cost prediction, particularly where past operating conditions have changed, or new conditions exist.

- The cost accounting distinction between fixed and variable costs and the simplifying assumption of linear variable costs may be reconciled with the economists' curvilinear cost model, provided that the *relevant range of activity* is considered.

Questions for review

1 Why is it important for the cost accountant to understand cost behaviour?

2 Define a variable cost and give *three* examples.

3 Define a fixed cost and give *three* examples.

4 Illustrate with the aid of a graph a variable cost.

5 Illustrate with the aid of a graph a fixed cost.

6 Demonstrate with the aid of a graph the linear cost function $y = a + b(x)$.

7 Discuss the advantages and disadvantages of the following methods for distinguishing between different cost classifications:

   a High/low method
   b Scattergraph
   c Least squares regression analysis

8 Give *three* examples of factors other than classification of costs, which may influence future costs.

9 Discuss the inconsistency of the accounting model and the economists' model for variable costs.

10 Demonstrate with the aid of a graph a curvilinear cost function.

11 What is the *relevant range of activity?*

Self-assessment questions

(*Denotes that a suggested solution may be found at the end of this book.)

1* Cost prediction

The data below relates to the transactions of Bank Ltd, a company engaged in the financial services industry

Period	No. of transactions (x)	Total cost (£) (y)
1	650	675
2	800	825
3	925	950
4	850	875
5	760	785

Using the high/low method, what costs should be expected in period 6 if output is:

a 700 transactions

b 850 transactions?

2 Cost prediction

Using the least squares regression method, determine the fixed and variable cost element from the following data and plot the same onto a graph, using the equation $y = a + b(x)$.

Period	No. of transactions (x)	Total cost (£) (y)
1	650	1425
2	800	1725
3	925	1975
4	850	1825
5	760	1645
6	775	1675
7	350	825
8	440	1005

What costs should be expected in period 9 if activity is:

a 700 transactions

b 850 transactions?

3* Total cost function

Total cost may be expressed as $y = a + b(x)$.

When $a = 500$ and $b = 15$:

Determine the total cost at activity levels of 100, 150 and 200.

4* Simultaneous equations

Using the high/low method, solve the following using simultaneous equations to determine the fixed and variable cost components:

$$y \quad = a + b(x)$$
$$220 = a + b(20)$$
$$120 = a + b(10)$$

Chapter 4

Accounting for labour costs

Chapter objectives

Having studied this chapter you should be able to:

- understand the importance of labour costs;
- understand the principal remuneration methods that exist;
- define piecework;
- be able to demonstrate how time based systems operate;
- understand the significance of labour costs as a proportion of total cost;
- appreciate the benefits of incentive based labour remuneration methods;
- be aware of how labour cost data may be captured for subsequent use in the cost accounting system.

Introduction

The purpose of this chapter is to provide some understanding of the different types of labour cost and the significance of such costs for organisations.

An appreciation of how labour costs may vary at differing levels of activity within the organisation, as a consequence of differing levels of volume or activity (where volume refers to the production of units or service delivered), is paramount, because for many organisations a significant proportion of labour costs are likely to be variable costs.

The significance of labour costs

Labour costs have been a significant cost for many organisations in the past, with a large part of the cost associated with production or service delivery. They have been treated as direct costs for costing purposes, because they have tended to vary at differing levels of activity or volume within the organisation.

More recently, there has been a greater reliance on automation in production and technology in service delivery. As a consequence of this shift away from the use of direct labour and a change in the remuneration methods of direct labour, the proportion of labour costs that are variable has fallen, whilst the proportion that are fixed has increased. This clearly has implications for cost management.

An understanding of the different labour remuneration methods employed is important, as it may have a bearing on the classification of the labour cost which is necessary for the application of many aspects of cost accounting, including:

- the determination of costs for products or services,
- planning (budgeting),
- control,
- decision making,
- what-if analysis, reflecting changes in output or activity.

Distinguishing between different remuneration methods

Remuneration methods may be

- based upon the level of output achieved (where output can be measured easily) or some other easily measurable indicator of performance;
- based upon time worked.

Output or performance remuneration (piecework)

The intention of output or performance based remuneration systems is to encourage high productivity and a reduction in the cost per unit produced or service delivered. Such schemes reward labour on the basis of the number of units produced (or perhaps the number of customers served). The effect of such systems is that high productivity levels result in an increase in remuneration to employees and a reduction in total cost for the organisation as there would be a reduction in the overhead per unit of output (or some other measure of activity) given that production or activity has increased.

There are numerous output or performance based remuneration systems, many of them specific to the organisation concerned. Many such systems are combined with an hourly rate for employees to provide some stability in earnings.

Output or performance based remuneration systems are often referred to as *piecework* systems and may be for individuals or groups of employees working together.

EXAMPLE

1 An employee is paid £5 per hour and produces 10 units in an 8-hour day. Fixed overheads are £20 per day.

2 A piecework system is introduced, whereby employees are paid £4.20 per unit manufactured.

3 As a result of the incentive scheme, production increases to 12 units per day. Fixed overheads remain the same.

Original total cost

	(£)
Labour	40 (£5 × 8 hrs)
Overhead	20
Total cost	60
Cost per unit	6 (£60/10 units)

Incentive scheme total cost

	(£)
Labour	50.40 (£4.20 × 12 units)
Overhead	20.00
Total cost	70.40
Cost per unit	5.87 (£70.40/12 units)

Summary

- The cost per unit of production has fallen by approximately (£6.00 – £5.87) £0.13.
- The remuneration to the employee has increased from (£5 × 8 hr) £40 per day to (£4.20 × 12 units) £50.40 per day.

Piecework systems appraisal

The advantages of piecework systems are:

- they increase production;
- they increase employee remuneration;
- they reduce unit costs;
- they improve the competitive position of the organisation.

The criticisms of piecework systems are:

- systems can become complex to administer;
- there are difficulties in agreeing the remuneration per unit of output;
- there are difficulties in determining an unit of output in some service organisations.

Remuneration based upon time worked

The intention of time worked based remuneration systems is to pay employees on the basis of the number of hours worked up to a given number of hours. Beyond this point an enhanced rate of pay would be earned; the enhancement may depend upon the number of additional hours worked and when they were worked.

EXAMPLE

1 An employee is paid £5 per hour for a 37-hour week.

2 Additional hours are remunerated at 1.5 times the basic hourly rate.

3 Sundays and statutory holidays are remunerated at twice the basic hourly rate.

4 In week 6 an employee worked 45 hours which included 4 hours on Sunday.

Total cost

	(£)
Labour (basic rate)	185 (£5 × 37 hrs)
Labour (1.5 × basic rate)	30 ((1.5 × £5) × 4 hrs)
Labour (2 × basic rate)	40 ((2 × £5) × 4 hrs)
Total labour cost	255

Time worked systems appraisal

The advantages of time worked systems are:

● they are simple to operate;

● they are easy to understand.

The criticisms of time worked systems are:

● there is no productivity incentive;

● employees are paid for time rather than output;

● a high level of supervision is required;

● a highly motivated workforce is required.

Labour cost data

Labour cost data may be captured as a by-product of the process of data collection for payroll. For payroll purposes sufficient information would have to be recorded for the period, which would enable correct payment of wages. Each employee would have to record hours worked, at either a standard or enhanced rate, for time worked systems, or the number of units produced, for piecework systems, or a combination of both for hybrid systems. This information could be captured electronically as employees work on a production line, or as a consequence of 'clocking on' using a time clock, or merely by completing a timesheet detailing this information.

It is worth mentioning that direct labour cost would also have other costs associated with it that would be included as part of the production overhead. Such costs include:

- overtime premiums, where additional payment has been made for manufacturing normal production;
- shift work premiums, where additional payment has been made for manufacturing normal production;
- National Insurance and pension contributions. Such costs are recorded as production overhead and an average rate determined and added to the direct costs;
- idle time, where production time has been lost, possibly due to poor production scheduling or equipment malfunction.

Summary

- Direct labour costs are a significant cost for many organisations.
  - A large proportion of labour cost is associated with production or service delivery.

- Remuneration methods may be based upon:
  - the level of output achieved,
  - hours worked.

- Output or performance based remuneration systems are often referred to as *piecework* systems.
  - Piecework systems may be for individuals or groups of employees working together.

- Time worked based remuneration systems pay employees on the basis of the number of hours worked up to a given number of hours.
  - Beyond this point an enhanced rate of pay would be earned by the employees.

- Labour cost data may be captured as part of the process of data collection for payroll purposes.
  - Such information could be captured via a variety of systems that record timesheet and productivity information.

- Other costs associated with direct labour cost, which may be included as a part of manufacturing are:
  - overtime premiums,
  - shift work premiums,
  - National Insurance and pension contributions,
  - idle time.

Questions for review

1 Discuss how information on labour costs may be obtained for the cost accounting system.

2 Explain a piecework system of remuneration.

3 Explain a time worked system of remuneration.

4 Illustrate with the aid of an example, how a piecework system may lower costs per unit whilst at the same time increasing remuneration to the employee.

5 Give *three* advantages of an incentive based labour remuneration system.

6 Give *two* disadvantages of an incentive based labour remuneration system.

7 Give *two* advantages of a time based remuneration system.

8 Give *two* disadvantages of a time based remuneration system.

9 Discuss how, for some organisations, the significance of labour costs has declined in recent years.

10 Give *three* examples of other costs associated with direct labour that could be classified as manufacturing overheads.

Self-assessment questions

(*Denotes that a suggested solution may be found at the end of this book.)

1* Piecework scheme

An employee is paid £5.50 per hour and produces 10 units in a 9-hour day. Fixed overheads are £200 per 5-day week.

A piecework system is introduced, whereby employees are paid £5.50 per unit manufactured. As a result of the incentive scheme, production increases to 12 units per day. Fixed overhead remains the same.

Determine the total production cost for a week.

2 Discussion of remuneration systems

Discuss the advantages and disadvantages of incentive based labour remuneration methods compared to time based remuneration systems.

3* Remuneration based upon time worked

An employee is paid £6 per hour for a 35-hour week. Additional hours are remunerated at 1.25 times the basic hourly rate. Sundays and statutory holidays are remunerated at twice the basic hourly rate.

In week 4 the employee worked 40 hours that included 2 hours on Sunday. Determine the total labour cost for week 4.

Chapter 5

Accounting for material costs

Chapter objectives

Having studied this chapter you should be able to:

- understand the importance of material costing;
- calculate the cost of stores issues and closing stock valuations using FIFO, LIFO, average cost, replacement cost and standard cost;
- discuss the advantages and criticisms of FIFO, LIFO, average cost, replacement cost and standard cost as a method of material pricing and closing stock valuation;
- discuss the problems of accounting for material costs.

Introduction

The purpose of this chapter is to provide some understanding of how material costs are dealt with in the cost accounting system. Accounting for material costs is necessary in most manufacturing environments as such costs are traceable and are likely to be significant. In many service environments however, materials that are consumed as part of providing a service are likely to be less significant in terms of overall cost and more difficult to trace to cost units. For this reason such materials are likely to be included as overhead in such environments rather than a direct cost.

The system for accounting for material costs must facilitate the recording of material costs for specific cost units and also provide the basis for stock valuation at period end.

Any system for accounting for material costs must enable data to be collected promptly and accurately, whilst at the same time being easy to administer.

It must also be acknowledged that in today's complex manufacturing environments with companies placing great emphasis on the diversity of the product portfolio, many companies are likely to require a wide range of materials and components. A robust system for accounting for material costs may therefore be required.

What is material pricing?

Material pricing methods objectives are twofold:

- to charge to cost units on a realistic basis, the cost of materials consumed;
- to provide a fair and consistent basis for stock valuation.

The issues of material from stores will result in the recording of a transaction between the stores and the cost item consuming the material (possibly via a work-in-progress account) as follows:

- record the quantity and value of materials issued;
- reduce the amount of materials stock by the same amount.

The cost for a unit of material may be affected by various factors that may have to be reflected in the issue price of the material. Examples of such factors are:

- The stock level for a particular material or component is likely to be made up of many deliveries from suppliers, each delivery may be at a different price.
- It may subsequently be difficult physically to identify units of material or individual components from a particular delivery.
- Prices may fluctuate for bought in materials and components.

In accounting for material costs, material-pricing systems devised must, as mentioned above, enable data to be collected promptly and accurately, whilst at the same time be easy to administer. The following material pricing systems are widely used in practice.

First in first out (FIFO)

The first in first out (FIFO) method requires that stores issues are made at the price of the oldest stock units until all of these units are used up. Stores issues are then made at the price of the next oldest units.

- FIFO uses actual material costs for charging to cost units.
- FIFO results in the material costs charged to cost units being the oldest prices. This may result in product costs being distorted.
- FIFO will overvalue stocks (compared with LIFO, described below) as stocks will always be valued at the latest prices.

EXAMPLE

Using the following stores data, determine the materials issue price and the closing stock valuation as at 30 September, using the first in first out method.

Date	Receipt qty	Price (£)	Issue qty	Replacement cost (£ per unit)
17/09	100	1.50		
18/09			50	1.50
19/09	60	1.75		
20/09			70	1.70
21/09	20	1.70		
22/09	10	1.90		
23/09	20	1.80		
24/09			66	1.85

The agreed standard material price throughout the period was £1.75/unit.

Solution

Receipt/issue date	Quantity	Price (£)	Issue details (£)	Balance (£)
17/09	100	1.50		$100 \times 1.50 = £150$
18/09	50		$50 \times 1.50 = £75$	$50 \times 1.50 = £75$
19/09	60	1.75		$50 \times 1.50 = £75$ $60 \times 1.75 = £105$
20/09	70		$50 \times 1.50 = £75$ $20 \times 1.75 = £35$ $£110$	$40 \times 1.75 = £70$
21/09	20	1.70		$40 \times 1.75 = £70$ $20 \times 1.70 = £34$
22/09	10	1.90		$40 \times 1.75 = £70$ $20 \times 1.70 = £34$ $10 \times 1.90 = £19$
23/09	20	1.80		$40 \times 1.75 = £70$ $20 \times 1.70 = £34$ $10 \times 1.90 = £19$ $20 \times 1.80 = £36$
24/09	66		$40 \times 1.75 = £70.00$ $20 \times 1.70 = £34.00$ $6 \times 1.90 = £11.40$ $£115.40$	$4 \times 1.90 = £7.60$ $20 \times 1.80 = £36.00$
30/09 Stock valuation				£43.60

Last in first out (LIFO)

The last in first out (LIFO) method requires that stores issues are made at the price of the most recent stock units until all of these units are used up. Stores issues are then made at the price of the next most recent units. Therefore each time new units are received into stock, this becomes the immediate issue price.

- LIFO uses actual material costs for charging to cost units.
- LIFO results in the material costs charged to cost units being more up to date prices.
- LIFO will undervalue stocks (compared with FIFO) as stocks will always be valued at the earliest prices.

EXAMPLE

Using the stores data from the previous example, determine the materials issue price and the closing stock valuation as at 30 September, using the last in first out method.

Solution

Receipt/issue date	Quantity	Price (£)	Issue details (£)	Balance (£)
17/09	100	1.50		$100 \times 1.50 = £150$
18/09	50		$50 \times 1.50 = £75$	$50 \times 1.50 = £75$
19/09	60	1.75		$50 \times 1.50 = £75$ $60 \times 1.75 = £105$
20/09	70		$60 \times 1.75 = £105$ $10 \times 1.50 = £15$ $£120$	$40 \times 1.50 = £60$
21/09	20	1.70		$40 \times 1.50 = £60$ $20 \times 1.70 = £34$
22/09	10	1.90		$40 \times 1.75 = £70$ $20 \times 1.70 = £34$ $10 \times 1.90 = £19$
23/09	20	1.80		$40 \times 1.75 = £70$ $20 \times 1.70 = £34$ $10 \times 1.90 = £19$ $20 \times 1.80 = £36$
24/09	66		$20 \times 1.80 = £36$ $10 \times 1.90 = £19$ $20 \times 1.70 = £34$ $16 \times 1.75 = £28$ $£117$	$24 \times 1.75 = £42$
30/09 Stock valuation				£42

Average cost (AVCO)

The average cost (AVCO) method requires that stores issues are made on a weighted average basis, whereby the issue price is recalculated each time new units are received. All units are issued at the average price until further units are received.

- AVCO does not use actual material costs for charging to cost units, but an average.
- AVCO results in more consistent material costs being charged to cost units. This may result in less product costs distortion.
- AVCO will value stocks differently to FIFO and LIFO as stocks will always be valued at the weighted average price.

EXAMPLE

Using the same stores data as above, determine the materials issue price and the closing stock valuation as at 30 September, using the average cost method.

Solution

Receipt/issue date	Quantity	Price (£)	Issue details (£)	Balance (£)
17/09	100	1.50		$100 \times 1.50 = £150$
18/09	50		$50 \times 1.50 = £75$	$50 \times 1.50 = £75$
19/09	60	1.75		$110 \times 1.64 = £180.40$ (W1)
20/09	70		$70 \times 1.64 = £114.80$	$40 \times 1.64 = £65.60$
21/09	20	1.70		$60 \times 1.66 = £99.60$ (W2)
22/09	10	1.90		$70 \times 1.69 = £118.30$ (W3)
23/09	20	1.80		$90 \times 1.71 = £153.90$ (W4)
24/09	66		$66 \times 1.71 = £112.86$	$24 \times 1.71 = £41.04$
30/09 Stock valuation				£41.04

Workings

(W1)
$$
\begin{array}{ll}
& \pounds \\
50 \text{ stock units} \times \pounds1.50 = & 75 \\
60 \text{ stock units} \times \pounds1.75 = & 105 \\
\hline
110 & 180 \\
\end{array}
$$

180/110 units = £1.636 363 6 (rounded to) **£1.64**

(W2)
$$
\begin{array}{ll}
& \pounds \\
40 \text{ stock units} \times \pounds1.64 = & 65.60 \\
20 \text{ stock units} \times \pounds1.70 = & 34.00 \\
\hline
60 & 99.60 \\
\end{array}
$$

99.60/60 units = **£1.66**

(W3)
$$
\begin{array}{ll}
& \pounds \\
60 \text{ stock units} \times \pounds1.66 = & 99.60 \\
10 \text{ stock units} \times \pounds1.90 = & 19.00 \\
\hline
70 & 118.60 \\
\end{array}
$$

118.60/70 units = £1.694 285 7 (rounded to) **£1.69**

(W4)
$$
\begin{array}{ll}
& \pounds \\
70 \text{ stock units} \times \pounds1.69 = & 118.30 \\
20 \text{ stock units} \times \pounds1.80 = & 36.00 \\
\hline
90 & 154.30 \\
\end{array}
$$

154.30/90 units = £1.714 444 4 (rounded to) **£1.71**

Replacement cost

The replacement cost method requires that stores issues be made at the current replacement cost of the units. In this way, stores issues price is designed to reflect the market value of a stock item.

- Replacement cost uses up-to-date material costs for charging to cost units.
- Replacement cost results in the material costs charged to cost units being current prices.
- Replacement costs must be determined for each stores issue.

EXAMPLE

Using the given stores data, determine the materials issue price and the closing stock valuation as at 30 September, using the replacement cost method.

45

Solution

Receipt/issue date	Quantity	Price (£)	Issue details (£)	Balance (£)
17/09	100	1.50		$100 \times 1.50 = £150$
18/09	50		$50 \times 1.50 = £75$	$50 \times 1.50 = £75$
19/09	60	1.75		$110 \times 1.75 = £192.50$
20/09	70		$70 \times 1.70 = £119$	$40 \times 1.70 = £68$
21/09	20	1.70		$60 \times 1.70 = £102$
22/09	10	1.90		$70 \times 1.90 = £133$
23/09	20	1.80		$90 \times 1.80 = £162$
24/09	66		$66 \times 1.85 = £122.10$	$24 \times 1.85 = £44.40$
30/09 Stock valuation				£44.40

Standard cost

The standard cost method requires that stores issues be made at a predetermined standard price that has been agreed in advance. In this way, stores issues price will remain constant for a stock item.

- Standard cost does not use up-to-date or actual material costs for charging to cost units.
- Standard cost results in the material costs charged to cost units being constant prices. This prevents changes in the issue price distorting product costs.
- Once standard costs are devised, the system is very simple to operate.

EXAMPLE

Using the stores data from the FIFO method example, determine the materials issue price and the closing stock valuation as at 30 September, using the standard cost method.

Solution

Receipt/issue date	Quantity	Price (£)	Issue details (£)	Balance (£)
17/09	100	1.75		$100 \times 1.75 = £175$
18/09	50		$50 \times 1.75 = £87.50$	$50 \times 1.75 = £87.50$
19/09	60	1.75		$110 \times 1.75 = £192.50$
20/09	70		$70 \times 1.75 = £122.50$	$40 \times 1.75 = £70$
21/09	20	1.75		$60 \times 1.75 = £105$
22/09	10	1.75		$70 \times 1.75 = £122.50$
23/09	20	1.75		$90 \times 1.75 = £157.50$
24/09	66		$66 \times 1.75 = £115.50$	$24 \times 1.75 = £42$
30/09 Stock valuation				£42

Use of different pricing methods

Each pricing method has advantages and disadvantages and each may result in different material costs being charged to cost units. It is therefore important that the method chosen is suitable for the organisation and for the conditions under which it will have to operate. In addition the pricing method chosen should be applied consistently and not changed from period to period. This will facilitate ease of comparison of subsequent performance data.

Stock valuation

The consequence of applying a particular material pricing method is that the closing stock valuation will be affected. This may have profit implications if this stock valuation is used as the basis for calculating business profit for external reporting.

For external reporting, it may be necessary to adjust the stock valuation to reflect a true and fair view in the financial accounts. There are specific regulatory requirements for stock valuation and reporting which require an organisation to value the stock at the lower of cost (i.e. all costs in getting the stock to its present location and condition) and net realisable value (sales proceeds less any costs of disposal).

Treatment of other costs

The cost of materials refers to all costs for the material in its present location and condition and may include such costs as

- delivery charges
- storage charges
- packaging charges
- quantity discounts.

Some costs should be specifically excluded from the cost of the material, such as

- VAT (as this cost is a recoverable tax);
- cash discount for early settlement of invoices.

There are also some costs, which do relate to the material costs, but may be insignificant or may not be easily identified to a unit of material. In such instances, the cost may be included as overhead.

Just-in-time

It is appropriate to briefly mention the Japanese management philosophy of just-in-time (JIT) that has recently become more popular in the West.

The approach involves the reduction of stockholding to identify waste and inefficiencies that stores may conceal. The consequence of no buffer stock is that material must arrive in the right quantities and be of the right quality and specification just in time for it to be used.

Significant benefits have been claimed for this method, including:

- reduction in working capital in stores,
- reduction of materials handling,
- more efficient ordering of material,
- fewer defective components supplied.

As a consequence of JIT, stores practices may need to change. The method for recording material pricing may also be simplified. LIFO, FIFO and AVCO material prices are likely to be similar as the material to be issued will be purchased and issued immediately before it is required. The method of material pricing may be less significant for those companies that adopt a JIT approach.

Summary

- Any system for accounting for material costs must:
  - facilitate the recording of material costs for specific cost units;
  - provide the basis for stock valuation at period end.

- Many companies are likely to require a wide range of materials and components to satisfy a diverse product portfolio.
  - A simple and robust system for accounting for material costs is required.

- The issues of material from stores will result in the recording of a transaction between the stores and the cost item consuming the material (possibly via a work-in-progress account) to:
  - record the quantity and value of materials issued;
  - reduce the amount of materials stock by the same amount.

- The following material pricing systems are widely used in practice:
  - FIFO,
  - LIFO,
  - AVCO,
  - replacement cost,
  - standard cost.

- Each material pricing method may result in different material costs being charged to cost units.
  - The pricing method chosen should be applied consistently.

- The particular material pricing method used will determine closing stock valuation.
  - This may have profit implications if this stock valuation is used as the basis for calculating business profit.
  - For external reporting, there are specific regulatory requirements for stock valuation.

- Just-in-time involves the reduction of stockholding to identify waste and inefficiencies that stores may conceal. Benefits claimed to be derived through JIT include:
  - reduction in working capital in stores,
  - reduction of materials handling,
  - more efficient ordering of material,
  - fewer defective components supplied.

Questions for review

1 Why is it important for the cost accountant to account for material costs?

2 Illustrate with the aid of an example the FIFO material pricing system.

3 Illustrate with the aid of an example the LIFO material pricing system.

4 Illustrate with the aid of an example the AVCO material pricing system.

5 Discuss the advantages and disadvantages of the following methods for material pricing:
   a FIFO
   b LIFO
   c AVCO
   d Standard cost
   e Replacement cost

6 Give *two* examples of costs that would not be recorded as part of the material cost.

7 Give *two* examples of costs that would be recorded as part of the material cost.

8 Describe the effect inflation would have on the closing stock valuation under the following material pricing systems:
   a FIFO
   b LIFO
   c AVCO
   d Standard cost
   e Replacement cost

9 Define 'standard price'.

10 Define 'replacement cost'.

11 Suggest reasons why material pricing systems may be inappropriate for stock valuation for financial reporting.

12 Discuss the Japanese management approach to stock levels and highlight the benefits that may ensue.

Self-assessment questions

(*Denotes that a suggested solution may be found at the end of this book.)

1* Stores issues and closing stock valuations
The following stores data represents the transactions for August.

Date	Receipt qty	Price (£)	Issue qty	Replacement cost (£ per unit)
17/08	150	1.50		
18/08			55	1.50
19/08	120	1.75		
20/08			70	1.70
21/08	25	1.70		
22/08	12	1.45		
23/08	22	1.80		
24/08			75	1.87

The agreed standard material price throughout the period was £1.65/unit.

Using the stores data above, determine the materials issue price and the closing stock valuation as at 31 August using the following material pricing systems:

a FIFO
b LIFO
c AVCO
d Standard cost
e Replacement cost

2 Differentiating material costs and overhead

Determine which of the following costs should be included as part of the material cost per unit and which costs, if any, could be considered as overhead.

a Delivery costs
b Storage costs
c Packaging costs
d Quantity discounts
e VAT
f Cash discounts

Chapter 6

Absorption costing

Chapter objectives

Having studied this chapter you should be able to:

- explain the rationale for the utilisation of absorption costing;
- understand the importance of absorption costing;
- define overhead allocation;
- understand the principles of apportionment;
- select appropriate bases of absorption;
- calculate overhead absorption rates;
- demonstrate the principles of absorption costing;
- understand the difference between service departments and production departments and their respective treatment;
- calculate a total product cost using an absorption costing approach;
- discuss the advantages and disadvantages of absorption costing.

Introduction

The purpose of this chapter is to introduce conventional full *absorption costing* systems, where overhead is unitised and included as part of the product or service in order that total cost (i.e. both fixed and variable costs) may be determined. The treatment of overhead, i.e. the manner in which it is incorporated into the product or service, is important in assessing product or service performance or profitability and may also have implications for pricing, where a full cost plus mark up formula is used in establishing a selling price.

It is, however, acknowledged that whilst the inclusion of overhead into each unit of product or service may be of value for the purpose of external reporting, its value is limited in decision making, where only variable costs would be considered. In these circumstances it may be more appropriate to adopt a *marginal costing* approach. This is discussed in Chapter 8.

Contemporary developments in management accounting have resulted in some criticism of absorption costing techniques. To overcome some of these apparent deficiencies, *activity based costing* was developed and is widely used as an alternative. This is discussed in Chapter 7.

What is absorption costing?

Absorption costing attempts to unitise overhead thereby including a proportion of the fixed cost incurred into each unit of production or service. In this way the cost of a unit of production or service will represent the full cost (i.e. both the fixed and variable costs). Absorption costing is required for all financial accounting statements used for the purpose of external reporting.

Overheads and absorption costing

You will recall from Chapter 2 that overhead refers to all costs except direct labour, direct materials and direct expenses. Examples of overhead costs are indirect costs, machinery costs, establishment costs, selling and distribution, administration and financial costs. In determining the full (or total) cost of a product or service, both the direct (variable) costs and overheads (fixed costs) must be determined. Direct cost information could be obtained from (say) materials requisitions and labour timesheets. Overheads, however, are likely to prove more problematic as they are not so readily identifiable to cost units. For example, it is difficult to determine the appropriate amount of the works manager's salary to charge to a single cost unit, particularly if some cost units take longer than others to complete.

The absorption costing process involves allocation, apportionment and finally absorption of overheads using predetermined overhead absorption rates (OAR). This will be discussed more fully later in this chapter.

The bases of absorption and absorption rates

The purpose of the overhead absorption system is to determine the total cost of a product or service, including a share of the overhead. It is acknowledged that in any attempt to share out a fixed cost over the total production capacity, there will be some loss of accuracy, as there is little if any linear relationship between overhead costs and the number of units produced. (See Chapter 3, 'Cost behaviour'). However, the emphasis of absorption costing is on being just and equitable with the amount of overhead charged to a cost unit and this should reflect the amount of time or effort spent on a particular unit of production.

Overhead costs are for a given period of time. Productive capacity may also be measured over the same period of time. With this in mind overhead costs may be charged to items produced in proportion to the production capacity consumed in making each item.

Production capacity may take the form of

- direct labour hours
- machine hours
- total units produced
- total direct wages
- total direct material

or some other *base* that adequately measures production capacity.

Once production capacity is determined and quantified, possibly using one of the bases outlined above, an overhead absorption rate may be determined based upon the following

$$\frac{\text{Total overhead}}{\text{Total amount of production capacity measure}} = \text{OAR}$$

EXAMPLE

A company producing washing machines has estimated the following cost and production data for a single period:

Total overhead		£80,000
	£	Hours
Direct labour	25,000	5,000
Machinery	40,000	16,000

Using this data, the following absorption rates may be determined:

- **Direct labour hours OAR**

$$\frac{80,000 \text{ (overhead)}}{5,000 \text{ (direct labour hours)}} = \pounds 16 \text{ per direct labour hour}$$

- **Machinery hours OAR**

$$\frac{80,000 \text{ (overhead)}}{16,000 \text{ (machinery hours)}} = \pounds 5 \text{ per machine hour}$$

- **Direct labour cost OAR**

$$\frac{80,000 \text{ (overhead)}}{25,000 \text{ (direct labour cost)}} = \pounds 3.20 \text{ per } \pounds 1 \text{ of direct labour cost}$$

- Machinery cost OAR

$$\frac{80{,}000 \text{ (overhead)}}{40{,}000 \text{ (machinery cost)}} = £2 \text{ per £1 of machinery cost}$$

The direct cost of one washing machine is £125. Assuming overhead is absorbed on the basis of direct labour hours and it requires 4 hours of labour time to manufacture a washing machine, determine the total product cost.

Solution

	£	
Direct cost	125	
Overhead	64	(4 hrs × £16)
Total cost	189	

How many washing machines will need to be made and sold to recover all overheads?

Solution

$$\frac{£80{,}000}{£64} = 1{,}250 \text{ washing machines}$$

In this example overhead was absorbed into the product on the basis of the number of labour hours. This is the most common basis in practice, but the base selected should reflect the amount of overhead likely to be incurred by a cost unit and should, as mentioned above, reflect the amount of time or effort spent on a particular unit of production. The factors that should be borne in mind when selecting an appropriate base are:

- The level of labour intensity in production. A direct labour hour basis would be most appropriate here.
- The level of mechanisation in production. A machine hour basis would be more appropriate here.
- The production is homogeneous. Where all production units are identical and are made in exactly the same way a cost per unit basis would suffice.
- The complexity of production. Where production processes are very complex, with a diversity of products, *activity based costing* may be more appropriate than absorption costing. Cost drivers replace the bases for absorption. This is discussed in Chapter 7.

FURTHER EXAMPLE

A product passes through three production departments: shaping, machining and final assembly. Their respective overhead costs together with details and appropriate basis for absorption are as follows:

	£ overhead	Absorption base
Shaping dept	25,000	5,000 (labour hours)
Machining dept	30,000	15,000 (machine hours)
Final assembly	40,000	10,000 (units produced)

Details of direct costs per unit of production for each department are as follows:

	Direct labour (£/unit)	Direct material (£/unit)
Shaping dept	50	15
Machining dept	35	45
Final assembly	21	55

The overhead absorption rates for each of the departments have been determined as follows:

- **Shaping dept: direct labour hours OAR**

$$\frac{25,000 \ (\text{overhead})}{5,000 \ (\text{direct labour hours})} = £5 \text{ per direct labour hour}$$

- **Machining dept: machinery hours OAR**

$$\frac{30,000 \ (\text{overhead})}{15,000 \ (\text{machine hours})} = £2 \text{ per machine hour}$$

- **Final assembly unit cost OAR**

$$\frac{40,000 \ (\text{overhead})}{10,000 \ (\text{units produced})} = £4 \text{ per unit produced}$$

If the product takes 4 hours of labour time in the shaping department and 3 hours of machine time in the machinery department before being finished in the final assembly department, determine the total product cost.

Solution

- **Shaping dept costs:**

	£
Direct labour	50
Direct material	15
Overhead	20 (4 hrs × £5)
Total cost	85

- Machining dept costs:

	£
Direct labour	35
Direct material	45
Overhead	6 (3 hrs × £2)
Total cost	**86**

- Final assembly costs:

	£
Direct labour	21
Direct material	55
Overhead	4 (£4 × 1 unit)
Total cost	**80**

- Total product cost:

	£
Shaping dept	85
Machining dept	86
Final assembly	80
Total cost	**251**

Over/under absorption of overhead

Overhead is included into cost units using predetermined overhead absorption rates of the type outlined in our first illustration of bases of absorption. These absorption rates are determined in advance using estimates of overhead cost and activity (e.g. labour hours, machine hours etc.).

It is unlikely that our estimates for overhead cost will exactly coincide with actual cost. The same will be the case for (say) the number of labour hours or machine hours. This may result in more or less overheads being absorbed into production than have actually been incurred. The former is referred to as *over absorption*, the latter as *under absorption*.

EXAMPLE

Using the data from our first illustration of bases of absorption determine the over/under absorption, assuming that actual overhead cost is £78,000 and production was only 1200 washing machines in the period, with overhead absorbed on a direct labour hour basis.

Solution

	£
Overhead absorbed	76,800 ((4 hrs × £16) × 1200 machines)
Overhead actual	78,000
Under absorption	**1,200**

The amount of £1200 of under absorbed overheads would be determined at the end of the period and would be included in the profit and loss account before any profit calculation is undertaken. In this case the profit for the period would be £1200 lower than anticipated, as this is the amount of overhead that has been incurred, but not charged to units of production.

The inclusion of overhead into cost units via cost centres

The most common method of charging overhead to cost units involves a two-stage process (see Figure 14). Overhead is first charged to cost centres, which were defined in Chapter 2 as an intermediate stage where costs may be gathered for later distribution. A cost centre could be a department, location, person etc. Once overheads are charged to cost centres they may then be applied to cost units. This process involves:

- **Allocation**   Where a cost may be clearly identified with a cost centre it may be allocated without splitting or division.

- **Apportionment**   Where a cost cannot be allocated to a cost centre it may be apportioned (shared out) between two or more cost centres.

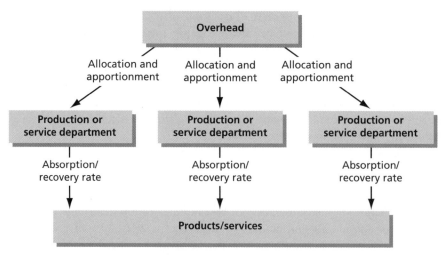

Figure 14 A two-stage method of charging overhead to cost units

- **Absorption** Where overhead has been allocated and apportioned to cost centres, it may be applied to a cost unit using a predetermined absorption (recovery) rate as illustrated in our bases of absorption examples above.

Two-stage method – illustration

A company has three production departments and one service department. They are divided into the following four cost centres:

- machining (M)
- assembly (A)
- finishing (F)
- stores (S).

The following cost data has been extracted from the accounts for period 6.

- **Allocated costs** These costs have been clearly identified with a cost centre and have been allocated without splitting or division.

	M £	A £	F £	S £
Indirect materials	2,800	3,000	2,600	–
Indirect wages	1,200	1,000	1,400	3,000
Total	4,000	4,000	4,000	3,000

- **Overhead costs requiring apportionment** These costs cannot be allocated to a cost centre so require apportionment between the cost centres on a fair basis.

	£
Rent	3,000
Rates	2,500
Light and heat	4,600
Building repairs	5,500
Plant depreciation	6,200
Total	21,800

- **Other information** For calculation of apportionments and absorption rates.

	M	A	F	S
Area occupied (m²)	1,300	3,200	2,500	1,000
Plant cost £	4,800	7,300	6,700	4,200
Direct labour hours	3,000	1,000	750	–
Machine hours	2,100	2,200	1,900	–
No. of stores requisitions	50	150	50	–

In order that the overhead absorption rate may be determined for each cost centre:

1 All overheads that cannot be allocated must be apportioned to production and service departments.

Allocated overhead

	M £	A £	F £	S £
Indirect materials	2,800	3,000	2,600	–
Indirect wages	1,200	1,000	1,400	3,000
Sub-total	4,000	4,000	4,000	3,000

Apportioned overhead

	M £	A £	F £	S £
Rent (W1)	487.50	1,200.00	937.50	375.00
Rates (W1)	406.25	1,000.00	781.25	312.50
Light and heat (W1)	747.50	1,840.00	1,437.50	575.00
Building repairs (W1)	893.75	2,200.00	1,718.75	687.50
Plant depreciation (W2)	2,100.00	2,200.00	1,900.00	–
Sub-total	4,635.00	8,440.00	6,775.00	1,950.00

Workings for apportionment

(W1) Apportioned according to proportion of floor space occupied (e.g. M: 16.25%; A: 40%; F: 31.25%; S: 12.5%)

(W2) Apportioned according to proportion of machine hours

Total allocated and apportioned overhead

	M £	A £	F £	S £
Sub-total: allocated	4,000	4,000	4,000	3,000
Sub-total: apportioned	4,635	8,440	6,775	1,950
Total	8,635	12,440	10,775	4,950

2 Once total allocated and apportioned overhead is determined, all service department costs must be reallocated to production cost centres.

Service departments do not produce units, but provide support for other departments. As a consequence, no units of production would pass through a service department. Therefore the overhead from a service department (in this case stores) must be apportioned to the production departments on a fair basis (in this case the number of stores requisitions).

	M £	A £	F £	S £
Total (as above)	8,635	12,440	10,775	4,950
Stores: apportioned (W3)	990	2,970	990	(4,950)
Total	9,625	15,410	11,765	–

Workings for apportionment

(W3) Apportioned according to proportion of stores requisitions (e.g. M: 20%; A: 60%; F: 20%)

3 Once all service department costs are reallocated to production cost centres, a separate overhead absorption rate may be calculated for each production department.

The absorption rate in this case has been determined on the basis of machine hours for cost centre M, as the majority of overheads are likely to be associated to machine hours. Whereas for cost centres A and F, which are unlikely to be machine intensive, labour hours have been used as the base for absorption. In practice the choice of absorption base may be somewhat subjective, resulting in a possibly questionable rate.

	M £	A £	F £
Total (as above)	9,625	15,410	11,765
Direct labour hours	3,000	**1,000**	750
Machine hours	**2,100**	2,200	1,900
OAR	4.58 (W4)	15.41 (W5)	15.69 (W6)

Workings for absorption rate

(W4) $\dfrac{£9,625}{2,100} = £4.583\,33$ rounded to £4.58

(W5) $\dfrac{£15,410}{1000} = £15.41$

(W6) $\dfrac{£11,765}{750} = £15.6866$ rounded to £15.69

4 Once absorption rates have been determined, they may be applied to products according to the basis used for each cost centre as illustrated in our second bases of absorption example (e.g. the number of machine hours worked on a unit of production in cost centre M, or the number of labour hours worked on a unit of production in cost centres A and F).

If one unit of production spent two hours in the machining department, three hours in the assembly department and one hour in the finishing department, the total overhead burden for the product would be:

Total overhead cost

	£
Machining dept	9.16 (2 hrs × £4.58)
Assembly dept	46.23 (3 hrs × £15.41)
Finishing dept	15.69 (1 hr × £15.69)
Total	71.08

The total overhead cost would be added to the direct costs to determine the overall product cost.

Non-manufacturing overhead

For the purpose of financial accounting, only manufacturing costs are allocated to products. Non-manufacturing overhead such as delivery costs are written off against profit in the same manner as the over/under recovery of overhead. For cost accounting it is possible to include such expenses as part of the product cost using absorption costing, however it is not common as the bases used for apportionment of non-manufacturing overheads tend to be quite arbitrary and result in very subjective absorption rates.

Appraisal of absorption costing

Advantages
The following are claimed to be advantages of absorption costing:

- The process of establishing cost centres provides a useful point for planning and control of an organisation's operations.
- Total product costs are obtained in a just and equitable manner.

- Where companies utilise a cost plus formula as the basis for establishing selling prices, absorption costing provides data on which to base these selling prices.

Disadvantages

The following are claimed to be disadvantages of absorption costing:

- Agreeing all of the costs to be allocated to a particular cost centre may be problematical.
- There may be difficulties in determining the most appropriate base for apportionment.
- The accuracy of product costs under absorption costing is questionable given the arbitrary nature of apportionment.
- Overhead absorption rates tend to be based upon a simple measure of volume, such as labour or machine hours. This does not necessarily reflect the contemporary production environment.
- Total product cost information that includes both fixed and variable costs is unlikely to be suitable for decision making. A marginal costing approach (see Chapters 8 and 9) may be preferable.

Summary

- Absorption costing may be used for:
  - the determination of full cost for products or services.

- Absorption costing attempts to unitise overhead.
  - It includes a proportion of the fixed cost incurred into each unit of production.
  - The cost of a unit of production or service will represent the full cost.

- Overhead refers to all costs except direct labour, direct materials and direct expenses. Examples of overhead costs are:
  - indirect costs,
  - machinery costs,
  - establishment costs,
  - selling and distribution,
  - administration and financial costs.

- Overhead costs may be charged to items produced in proportion to the production capacity consumed in making each item, where production capacity refers to:
  - direct labour hours,

- machine hours,
- total units produced,
- total direct wages,
- total direct material.

- The factors that should be borne in mind when selecting an appropriate base for absorption of overhead are:
  - the level of labour intensity in production,
  - the level of mechanisation in production,
  - whether the production is homogeneous,
  - the complexity of production.

- It is unlikely that estimates for overhead cost will exactly coincide with the actual cost. This may also be the case for (say) the number of labour hours or machine hours.
  - The result is more or less overheads being absorbed into production than have actually been incurred. This is referred to as *over/under absorption.*

- The most common method of charging overhead to cost units involves a two-stage process:
  - overhead is first to be charged to cost centres,
  - overhead is then applied to cost units using OAR.

- The two-stage process involves the following steps:
  - Allocation   Where a cost may be clearly identified with a cost centre it may be allocated without splitting or division.
  - Apportionment   Where a cost cannot be allocated to a cost centre it may be apportioned (shared out) between two or more cost centres.
  - Reapportionment   All service department costs are reallocated to production cost centres.
  - Absorption   Once overhead has been allocated and apportioned to cost centres, it may be applied to a cost unit using a predetermined absorption (recovery) rate.

- For the purpose of financial accounting, only manufacturing costs are allocated to products.
  - Non-manufacturing overhead such as delivery costs are written off against profit in the same manner as the over/under recovery of overhead.

- Absorption costing facilitates the following:
  - total product costs obtained in a just and equitable manner,
  - where a cost plus formula is utilised for selling prices, data on which to base these selling prices.

- The limitations of absorption costing are:
  - The accuracy of product costs is questionable given the arbitrary nature of apportionment.
  - Overhead absorption rates rely on a simple measure of volume. This does not necessarily reflect the contemporary production environment.
  - Total product cost information that includes both fixed and variable costs is unlikely to be suitable for decision making.

Questions for review

1 Define absorption costing and give an example to illustrate this.

2 Explain the term full product cost.

3 Define the term cost centre and comment on its significance for absorption costing.

4 Define the following terms:
  a Allocation
  b Apportionment
  c Reapportionment
  d Absorption

5 Suggest possible bases for the absorption of overhead for a production cost centre.

6 Give *three* reasons why absorption costing may be beneficial to an organisation.

7 Give *four* limitations of absorption costing.

8 Discuss the reasons why an arbitrary process of apportionment is acceptable in pursuit of a just and equitable product cost.

9 Explain the difference between service departments and production departments and their respective treatment of overhead costs.

10 Using a diagram, illustrate the two-stage process for the inclusion of overhead into cost units via cost centres.

11 Give examples of overhead which may be allocated to a cost centre.

12 Give examples of overhead which may be apportioned to a cost centre.

13 Suggest bases of apportionment for the following overheads:
  a Rent
  b Buildings repairs
  c Plant depreciation
  d Factory administration

Self-assessment questions

(*Denotes that a suggested solution may be found at the end of this book.)

1* Absorption rates

A company producing fridges has estimated the following cost and production data for a single period:

Total overhead		£90,000
	£	Hours
Direct labour	20,000	4,000
Machinery	45,000	16,000

Using the above data, determine the following absorption rates:

a   Direct labour hours OAR
b   Machinery hours OAR
c   Direct labour cost OAR
d   Machinery cost OAR.

2* Total product cost

Using the data from Question 1, if the direct cost of one fridge is £12 and it takes 4 hours of labour time to manufacture it, determine the total product cost.

3* Overhead recovery

Using the data from Question 1, how many fridges will need to be made and sold to recover all overheads?

4* Allocation, apportionment and absorption

A company has three production departments and one service department. They are divided into the following four cost centres: machining (M), assembly (A), finishing (F) and stores (S).

The following cost data has been extracted from the accounts.

Allocated costs

	M	A	F	S
	£	£	£	£
Indirect materials	1,800	2,000	2,600	–
Indirect wages	1,200	1,000	2,400	3,000
Total	3,000	3,000	5,000	3,000

Overhead costs requiring apportionment

	£
Rent	3,500
Rates	2,500
Light and heat	4,650
Building repairs	5,500
Plant depreciation	5,200
Total	21,350

Other information

	M	A	F	S
Area occupied (m^2)	1,500	3,500	2,500	500
Plant cost £	4,800	7,300	6,700	4,250
Direct labour hours	3,000	1,250	1,750	–
Machine hours	1,000	2,000	2,000	–
No. of stores requisitions	50	100	100	–

a Determine the overhead absorption rate for:

   i.   Cost centre M using a direct labour hours basis
   ii. Cost centre A using a machine hours basis
   iii. Cost centre F using a direct labour hours basis.

b If one unit of production spent two hours in the machining department, two machine hours in the assembly department and three hours in the finishing department, determine the total overhead burden for the product.

c Determine the total product cost if direct costs are £25/unit.

5 Full product costs for selling prices

Discuss the deficiencies of a conventional absorption costing approach when used to determine the full cost of a product, which may be subsequently used as part of a cost plus formula for establishing a selling price.

Chapter 7

Activity based costing

Chapter objectives

Having studied this chapter you should be able to:

- explain the limitations of traditional absorption costing systems;
- discuss the difference between ABC systems and traditional absorption costing systems;
- understand the importance of ABC;
- illustrate the framework of ABC;
- understand the distinction between short-term and long-term variable overhead costs;
- explain the term cost driver;
- determine appropriate cost drivers;
- apply cost driver rates;
- calculate a total product cost using an ABC approach;
- discuss the advantages and disadvantages of ABC.

Introduction

The purpose of this chapter is to consider the deficiencies of conventional full *absorption costing* systems, where overhead is unitised and included as part of the product or service and to introduce an alternative approach to treating overhead within full costing systems, referred to as *activity based costing*, which arguably better reflects the sophistication of the manufacturing or service environment. As we have stated, the treatment of overhead, i.e. the manner in which it is incorporated into the product or service, is important in assessing product or service performance or profitability and may also have implications for pricing, where a full cost plus mark up formula is used in establishing a selling price.

Absorption costing principles were explained in Chapter 6, and will be demonstrated again in this chapter where we compare activity based costing (ABC) with traditional absorption costing.

What is activity based costing?

Activity based costing is a relatively new costing technique that emerged during the late 1980s. Its proponents, Professors Kaplan and Cooper, developed the technique in response to the spread of advanced manufacturing technology (AMT), which arguably rendered traditional absorption costing deficient for product cost information purposes. It is claimed that ABC provides better product cost information, by recognising and relating the overhead costs to the activities that cause or drive overhead. This will be discussed in more detail later on in this chapter. Activity based costing is also applicable to large-scale service organisations, where overheads are a significant cost. This will be discussed more fully below.

Advanced manufacturing technology (AMT)

In recent years, manufacturing has evolved, with the introduction of greater technology and more automation. Companies are now able to produce a wider range of products, with greater product variation, to respond to a more competitive and demanding marketplace.

In this advanced manufacturing technology environment, it is acknowledged that production processes are far more multifaceted, with companies producing an increasingly diverse range of products for a more sophisticated consumer. These products may differ in both volume and complexity. As a consequence, the cost structure of such companies has also changed, with direct costs now representing a smaller proportion of total cost than in the past, when material and labour costs were the dominant production expense.

With the improvement in manufacturing technology, production processes have also changed. These processes now tend to include costs for a variety of support activities, for example work scheduling, set ups for product variations, stock handling etc. Such costs may not increase with the volume of activity or output, but could vary with the range and complexity of the products manufactured. This will inevitably have implications for the costing method employed in determining the full cost of a product manufactured in such an environment.

The implications of AMT for ABC

Traditional absorption costing systems were designed at a time when the majority of companies had a narrow product range and the use of technology and automation as part of the production environment was limited. Direct labour and material costs were the dominant production costs and management's attention was primarily focused on these rather than the less significant overhead costs. Distortions in total product costs arising from absorption costing, where overhead was primarily included in the cost of the product via labour hours, machine

69

hours or a similar volume based approach, was not considered material, given the relative insignificance of overhead costs. In addition, the opportunities for sophisticated overhead allocation methods were limited given the high cost of information processing at the time.

Today, information processing costs have fallen by an order of magnitude, allowing cost effective complex analysis of overhead costs. This, coupled with the fact that in an AMT environment, direct costs now represent a smaller proportion of total costs and overhead has risen significantly with the greater use of technology in production and a more complex production environment, has provided an opportunity for the development of contemporary cost and management accounting techniques. As we have said, in an AMT environment overhead costs may not increase with the volume of activity or output, but could vary with the range and complexity of the products manufactured, and the greatest distortion in product costing using traditional absorption techniques is likely to occur under these circumstances. There is little if any relationship between overhead and machine hours or labour hours for many companies today, and arguably the recovery of overheads on this basis is futile and meaningless. Activity based costing was developed in an effort to overcome many of these deficiencies.

The implications of ABC for service organisations

Activity based costing is equally applicable to large-scale service organisations such as banks and hospitals, where a large proportion of overheads cannot be directly assigned and a wide variety of services are offered. The activities that cause or drive overheads will inevitably be different from manufacturing companies, but the framework of ABC remains the same and will be discussed later.

The benefits of ABC for service organisations are not dissimilar to manufacturing companies. Moreover, it is argued that the benefits may be greater than for manufacturing organisations, as the majority of costs in large-scale service organisations are likely to be fixed and therefore treated as overhead. Contrast this with manufacturing, where a significant proportion of total cost may be variable, given that direct materials and direct labour are likely to be traced to individual products.

Overhead

Classification of overhead using ABC

For ABC, the majority of overhead costs may be classified between:

- **short-term variable costs** which vary with the volume of production. These costs may be traced to products or services using measures of the volume of activity (e.g. machine hours, labour hours). Most organisations will have some overhead costs that could be classified as short-term variable costs;

- **long-term variable costs** which do not vary with the volume of production or service, but do vary with some other measure of activity. These costs may *not* be traced to products or services using measures of the volume of activity (as above), but would be associated with the transactions undertaken by the support departments where the costs are incurred. (For example, set-up costs, customer service costs, production scheduling, inspection costs, purchase costs, despatch costs).

Cost drivers

Activity based costing recognises the need to understand the behaviour of overhead costs and to identify what activities cause overhead costs to change. The essence of ABC is that activities cause cost, not the products themselves. Products, however, consume activities. The more activities consumed by a product, the greater the proportion of the overhead burden that should be borne by the product or service. Contrast this with traditional absorption costing where only the volume of production or service itself would increase the share of overhead to a product line. ABC attempts to overcome this potential shortfall by attempting to relate overhead costs to the activities that cause or 'drive' them. These are referred to as *cost drivers*.

- For short-term variable costs, the cost driver will be the volume of activity.
- For long-term variable costs, the cost driver will be related to transactions undertaken by support departments where the costs are incurred. Examples of support department costs and possible cost drivers are as follows:

Support department costs	Possible cost driver
Set-up costs	No. of set-ups
Production scheduling	No. of production runs
Inspection and quality costs	No. of inspections
Purchase costs	No. of purchase orders
Despatch costs	No. of deliveries
Production control	No. of set-ups

All of the costs associated with a particular cost driver (e.g. number of set-ups) would be grouped into a cost pool. Costs are grouped into pools on the basis of activity rather than on a departmental basis. These cost pools would be subsequently applied to a product line using cost driver rates (this is described in our ABC example below) with the number of transactions as the basis for the cost driver.

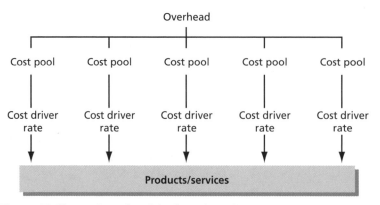

Figure 15 Illustration of activity based costing

Contrast this with traditional absorption costing, where all production overhead would be included in the product cost on the basis of a simple volume measure, the most common being the number of labour hours.

Framework of ABC

The framework of ABC may be summarised as follows:

- recognise the major activities of the organisation;
- determine the most appropriate *cost driver* for each major activity;
- group identical *cost drivers* into *cost pools*;
- include the cost of an activity into the product cost according to the product's use of each activity.

Illustration of ABC

EXAMPLE

A company manufactures two products P and Q, using the same equipment and identical processes. An extract of the production data for period 1 is as follows:

	P	Q
Quantity produced (units)	6,000	11,000
Direct labour hours/unit	1	2
Machine hours/unit	3	2
Set-ups in the period	10	30
Orders handled in the period	15	35

Overhead costs relating to:

	£
Machine activity	250,000
Production set-ups	30,000
Order handling	40,000
	320,000

Calculate the production overhead to be included in a unit of product P and Q using an activity based cost approach with the following cost drivers:

Support department costs	Cost driver
Machine activity	Machine hours
Production set-ups	No. of set-ups
Order handling	No. of orders

Solution

Overhead	£	Cost driver	Budgeted volume	Rate
Machine activity	250,000	Machine hrs	40,000 hrs (W1)	**£6.25/hr** (W2)
Production set-ups	30,000	Set-ups	40 set-ups (W3)	**£750/set-up** (W4)
Order handling	40,000	Orders	50 orders (W5)	**£800/order** (W6)

Workings

(W1) Product P: 6,000 units × 3 machine hrs/unit = 18,000 hrs
Product Q: 11,000 units × 2 machine hrs/unit = 22,000 hrs
40,000 hrs

(W2) £250,000/40,000 hrs = **£6.25 per hr**

(W3) Product P: 10 set-ups
Product Q: 30 set-ups
40 set-ups

(W4) £30,000/40 set-ups = **£750 per set-up**

(W5) Product P: 15 orders
Product Q: 35 orders
50 orders

(W6) £40,000/50 orders = **£800 per order**

Production overhead to be included in a unit of product P using an activity based cost approach:

	£
Machine driven costs	112,500 ((6000 units × 3 hrs) × £6.25)
Set-up costs	7,500 (£750 × 10 set-ups)
Order handling	12,000 (£800 × 15 orders)
	132,000
Units produced	6,000
Therefore, overhead/unit:	£22

Production overhead to be included in a unit of product Q using an activity based cost approach:

	£
Machine driven costs	137,500 ((11,000 units × 2 hrs) × £6.25)
Set-up costs	22,500 (£750 × 30 set-ups)
Order handling	28,000 (£800 × 35 orders)
	188,000
Units produced	11,000
Therefore, overhead/unit:	£17.09 (rounded)

EXAMPLE – comparison of abc and absorption costing

A company manufactures four products A, B, C, D. Output data for the period is as follows:

	A	B	C	D
No. of production runs	2	3	6	20
No. of set-ups	2	4	6	8
Output (units)	10	20	50	200
Labour hours/unit	1	2	1	2
Machine hours/unit	1	3	2	1

Cost data for the period is as follows:

	A	B	C	D
	£	£	£	£
Material cost/unit	20	60	40	80

Direct labour cost is £5 per hour.

Support department overhead costs, together with possible cost drivers, are as follows:

Support department costs	£	Possible cost driver
Set-up costs	20,000	No. of set-ups
Production scheduling	15,500	No. of production runs
Short run variable costs	7,500	Labour hours
Material handling	18,600	No. of production runs
	61,600	

Using an activity based costing approach, determine the total cost per unit for each of the four products. Recalculate this using traditional absorption costing (based upon labour hours).

Solution

ABC approach

	A	B	C	D
Material	200	1,200	2,000	16,000
Labour	50	200	250	2,000
Set-up costs (W1)	2,000	4,000	6,000	8,000
Production scheduling (W2)	1,000	1,500	3,000	10,000
Short-run variable costs (W3)	150	600	750	6,000
Material handling (W4)	1,200	1,800	3,600	12,000
	4,600	9,300	15,600	54,000
Units produced	10	20	50	200
Cost per unit	460	465	312	270

Workings
(W1) Set-up costs: £20,000/20 set-ups = **£1000 per set-up**
(W2) Production scheduling: £15,500/31 production runs = **£500 per run**
(W3) Short-run variable costs: £7500/500 labour hours = **£15 per hour**
(W4) Material handling: £18,600/31 production runs = **£600 per run**

Absorption cost approach

	A	B	C	D
Material	200	1,200	2,000	16,000
Labour	50	200	250	2,000
Overheads (W5)	1,232	4,928	6,160	49,280
	1,482	6,328	8,410	67,280
Units produced	10	20	50	200
Cost per unit	148.20	316.40	168.20	336.40

Workings

(W5) Overheads absorbed on the basis of labour hours:
      £61,600/500 labour hours = £123.20 per hour

Comparison and discussion

The ABC approach utilises a greater quantity and diversity of cost drivers compared with absorption costing, which relies only on a simple and usually single volume based rate. The ABC approach recognises that some activities are unrelated to volume by using allocation bases that are not related to output. It is argued that ABC cost driver rates should as a consequence associate more closely to the overhead and serve to provide more accurate and meaningful product costs.

Traditional absorption costing provides very different figures for unit product costs for products A, B, C and D:

	A	B	C	D
Activity based costing	460.00	465.00	312.00	270.00
Absorption costing	148.20	316.40	168.20	336.40
Difference	311.80	148.60	143.80	(66.40)

When compared with ABC, traditional absorption costing results in the following:

- It over-allocates overhead to high volume products and under-allocates overhead to low volume products.

- It over-allocates overhead to products that require more hours of work and under-allocates overhead to products that require fewer hours.

Appraisal of ABC

Advantages

The following are claimed to be advantages of ABC:

- In an AMT environment, it is recognised that production processes are far more complex and that direct labour costs are likely to be a less significant proportion of total product cost. ABC is able to acknowledge this complexity with multiple cost drivers, some of which are not volume based.

- In a service environment, the tracing of costs to service delivery may prove more problematic. The use of a variety of cost drivers is likely to provide superior cost information compared with a purely volume based approach to the inclusion of overhead.

- The process of ascertaining cost drivers provides an opportunity for reappraisal of operations carried out in the business.
- Cost management of overhead is achieved by coupling the costs to the activities that 'drive' or cause them.
- ABC focuses management's attention on the significant determinants of overhead cost.
- More realistic product costs are obtained.
- Where companies utilise a cost plus formula as the basis for establishing selling prices, ABC provides arguably more reliable data on which to base selling prices.

Disadvantages

The following are claimed to be disadvantages of ABC:

- There may be difficulties in determining the most appropriate cost drivers.
- Agreeing all of the costs associated with a particular cost driver for subsequent grouping into a cost pool may be problematical.
- A limited number of cost drivers are unlikely to fully explain the cost behaviour of several items within a cost pool.
- A comprehensive ABC system with several cost drivers and many cost pools inevitably has a cost associated with it. The benefits provided by ABC must outweigh the costs.
- In a service environment, the tracing of costs to service delivery may result in too many cost drivers being identified than is feasible to implement.

Summary

- Activity based costing may be used for:
  - the determination of full cost for products or services.

- The limitations of traditional absorption costing systems are:
  - They do not recognise the complex cost environment within which many companies operate.
  - They use only a volume related measure for the absorption of overhead into a product or service.
  - There is little if any relationship between overhead and the volume related measures for many companies today.

- In an AMT environment, direct costs now represent a smaller proportion of total costs and overhead has risen significantly with the greater use of technology in production.

- A more complex production environment has provided the opportunity for the development of ABC.
- Overhead costs may not increase with the volume of output, but with some other measure of activity.
- The greatest distortion of product costing is likely to occur when traditional absorption costing is used in this environment.

- It is claimed that ABC provides better product cost information.
  - ABC relates overhead to the activities that cause or drive them.

- ABC is also applicable to large-scale service organisations:
  - for example, banks and hospitals,
  - where a large proportion of overhead cannot be directly assigned,
  - where a wide variety of services are offered.

- The framework of ABC is as follows:
  - Recognise the major activities of the organisation.
  - Determine the most appropriate *cost driver* for each major activity.
  - Group identical cost drivers into *cost pools*.

- A short-term variable cost may be defined as:
  - a cost that varies with the volume of production. These costs may be traced to products or services using measures of the volume of activity (e.g. machine hours, labour hours).

- A long-term variable cost may be defined as:
  - a cost that does not vary with the volume of production or service, but does vary with some other measure of activity. These costs would be associated with transactions undertaken by support departments where the costs are incurred (e.g. set-up cost, production scheduling, inspection costs etc.).

- The essence of ABC is that activities cause cost, not the products themselves.
  - For short-term variable costs, the cost driver will be the volume of activity.
  - For long-term variable costs, the cost driver will be related to transactions undertaken by support departments where the costs are incurred.

- When compared with ABC, traditional absorption costing results in the following:
  - It over-allocates overhead to high volume products and under-allocates overhead to low volume products.
  - It over-allocates overhead to products that require more hours of work and under-allocates overhead to products that require fewer hours of work.

Questions for review

1 Define ABC and give an example to illustrate this.

2 What is an AMT environment? Explain the implications of such an environment for the cost accountant.

3 Define the term cost driver.

4 Explain the relationship between cost drivers and cost pools.

5 Discuss the difference between the two classifications of overhead of
   a Short-term variable costs
   b Long-term variable costs

6 Suggest possible cost drivers for the following support department costs:
   a Set-up costs
   b Production scheduling
   c Inspection and quality costs
   d Purchase costs
   e Despatch costs
   f Production control
   g Material planning

7 Give *three* reasons why ABC may lead to more realistic product costs.

8 Discuss the reasons for the difference in product costs recorded under ABC and absorption costing.

9 Comment on the implications of dissimilar product costs recorded under ABC and absorption costing for pricing and stock valuation.

10 Explain why traditional absorption costing, when compared with ABC, results in the following:
   a An over-allocation of overhead to high volume products and under-allocation of overhead to low volume products
   b An over-allocation of overhead to products that require more hours of work and an under-allocation of overhead to products that require fewer hours.

Self-assessment questions

(*Denotes that a suggested solution may be found at the end of this book.)

1* Product costs using ABC

A company manufactures two products L and H, using similar equipment and processes. An extract of the production data for period 6 is as follows:

	L	H
Quantity produced (units)	4,000	10,000
Direct labour hours/unit	1	2
Machine hours/unit	3	2
Set-ups in the period	10	30
Orders handled in the period	25	25

	L	H
	£	£
Direct labour cost/unit	2	2
Direct material cost/unit	3	4

Overhead costs relating to:

	£
Machine activity	200,000
Production set-ups	20,000
Engineering stores	40,000
	260,000

Determine appropriate cost drivers for the support department costs and calculate the total cost of a unit of product L and H using an activity based cost approach.

2 Product costs using ABC and absorption costing

A company manufactures four products P, Q, R and S. Output data for the period is as follows:

	P	Q	R	S
No. of production runs	4	3	6	20
No. of set-ups	2	4	6	8
Output (units)	10	20	50	100
Labour hours/unit	1	2	1	2
Machine hours/unit	1	3	2	1

Cost data for the period is as follows:

	P	Q	R	S
	£	£	£	£
Material cost/unit	40	60	40	60

Direct labour cost is £10 per hour.

Support department overhead costs, together with possible cost drivers are as follows:

Support department costs	£	Possible cost driver
Set-up costs	40,000	No. of set-ups
Production scheduling	15,500	No. of production runs
Short run variable costs	15,000	Labour hours
Material handling	18,600	No. of production runs
	89,100	

Using an activity based costing approach, determine the total cost per unit for each of the four products. Recalculate this using traditional absorption costing (based upon labour hours). Compare and discuss your findings.

3* Implementation of ABC

Discuss the features of a large-scale service organisation that would permit activity based costing to be implemented.

4 Reliability of full cost data

Discuss the assertion that activity based costing provides more reliable cost data on which to base pricing decisions.

Chapter 8

Marginal costing systems

Chapter objectives

Having studied this chapter you should be able to:

- understand the importance of marginal costing;
- explain the term marginal cost;
- calculate the marginal cost of an item;
- explain the term contribution;
- calculate contribution;
- understand the treatment of overhead under marginal costing;
- be able to demonstrate the differences for marginal costing and absorption costing in profit calculation;
- be able to calculate the breakeven point and margin of safety;
- be able to draw a breakeven graph;
- be able to draw a cost volume profit graph;
- appreciate the assumptions underlying marginal costing theory.

Introduction

The purpose of this chapter is to introduce an alternative approach to treating overhead within costing systems. As we have stressed, the treatment of overhead, i.e. the way it is incorporated into the product or service or the time period it relates to, is important in assessing product or service performance or profitability.

An understanding of the different types of cost and the distinct ways in which they behave under specified conditions was discussed in Chapter 3. It was at this stage that the fundamental classification of costs into fixed and variable was first introduced.

These cost classifications are utilised again in this chapter and the concept of contribution is also introduced.

Marginal costing may be used for:

- the determination of costs for products or services;

- the calculation of breakeven points;
- what-if analysis, reflecting changes in output or activity and the cost implications;
- as a short-run decision-making technique where the best use of existing capacity must be made. (This will be further addressed in Chapter 9.)

Marginal costing differs from full costing techniques such as *absorption costing* or *activity based costing* in the way in which it treats overhead. Using a marginal costing approach as opposed to a full costing method may result in a difference in the performance figures (profit) determined for the same data. However, such differences are recorded in the short term only and can be reconciled and explained by the ways that different techniques treat overhead. This will be explained more fully later on in the chapter.

What is marginal costing?

Marginal costing is the principle whereby only variable costs are charged to cost units for production or service. The fixed cost or overhead relating to the period where the production or service took place is written off in full against the *contribution* of that period. (Contribution will be explained below.)

Marginal cost

The marginal cost of a product or service is the variable costs of manufacture or service delivery.

Economists define marginal cost as 'the cost of the very last unit of production'. This definition is not inconsistent with the accountant's definition as the cost of the very last unit of production is the variable cost only. This definition may equally apply to service industries, with marginal cost referring to (say) the cost of the very last transaction in a bank, or (say) the very last swim in a swimming pool for a local authority.

Contribution

Contribution may be described as the difference between the sales revenue and the variable costs of those sales. It is the surplus after variable costs have been covered. For example,

	£
Sales	12,000
less Variable costs	(5,600)
Contribution	6,400

Contribution is relevant in many marginal costing calculations and is often described as a sub-total of profit, i.e. profit before the inclusion of fixed costs (overhead). Total fixed costs are set against the contribution. Once the fixed costs are covered the remaining contribution represents profit.

The treatment of overhead

Marginal costing treats overhead as a period cost, suggesting that overheads (rent, rates heat, light, power) do not relate to output or activity, but are incurred with the passage of time. For example, factory rent would remain the same irrespective of how many units were manufactured in the period. It follows that if there were no units manufactured, the rent would still have to be paid. Marginal costing writes off overhead in the period it is incurred irrespective of the level of production during the period.

Contrast this with absorption costing or activity based costing, where an attempt is made to unitise overhead and include a proportion of the overhead incurred into each unit of production (or some other measure of activity). In this way the cost of a unit of production or service will represent the full cost (i.e. both the fixed and variable costs). Absorption costing or activity based costing is required for all financial accounting statements used for the purpose of external reporting; for this purpose marginal costing will not suffice.

It is, however, acknowledged that whilst the inclusion of overhead into each unit of product or service may be of value for the purpose of external reporting, its value is limited in decision making, what-if analysis and breakeven analysis. In these circumstances it may be more appropriate to adopt a marginal costing approach.

Revenue statements in a marginal costing format

As discussed in Chapter 1, there is no law or statute governing the application of costing techniques, nor is there a legal requirement to produce cost accounting data using prescribed statements or formats. However, in the application of many costing techniques, preferred layouts have emerged over time. For marginal costing, the layout (with example data) is as follows:

	£
Sales	12,000
less Variable costs	(5,600)
Contribution	6,400
less Fixed costs	(5,000)
Profit	**1,400**

EXAMPLE

The following data was extracted from the accounts of a skateboard manufacturer:

	Total cost (£)	Fixed cost (£)	Variable cost (£)
Direct labour	1,700	1,500	200
Direct material	2,100	–	2,100
Overhead	1,900	1,840	60
	5,700	3,340	2,360

If 400 skateboards are manufactured and sold for £20 each in the period, determine the profit in a marginal costing format.

Solution

	£
Sales	8,000
less Variable costs	(2,360)
Contribution	5,640
less Fixed costs	(3,340)
Profit	**2,300**

You will recall from Chapter 3 that in the case of variable costs, there is a linear relationship between cost and output (or activity), unit variable costs remaining constant. We could therefore present the above statement on a *unit* basis as far as contribution.

	£	
Unit sales	20.00	
less Unit variable costs	(5.90)	(2360/400 units)
Unit contribution	14.10	
Total contribution	5,640	(£14.10 × 400 units)
less Fixed costs	(3,340)	
Profit	**2,300**	

The role of contribution

It is important to appreciate the central role that contribution plays in marginal costing theory. The use of contribution is helpful for decision making as it excludes fixed costs, which at best may only be shared arbitrarily between products/services. Contribution may be expressed per unit or in total.

EXAMPLE

Using the data from the example above, if 405 skateboards had been made and sold in the period, revenue variable costs and contribution would change as follows:

	£	
Sales	8,100.00	(£20.00 × 405 units)
less Variable costs	(2,389.50)	(£5.90 × 405 units)
Contribution	5,710.50	

The fixed costs (overhead) would remain unaltered. The profit, however, would increase to:

	£
Total contribution	5,710.50
less Fixed costs	(3,340.00)
Profit	**2,370.50**

The increase in profit of £2,370.50 – £2,300 = £70.50 is identical to the increase in contribution.

	£	
Contribution: 405 skateboards	5,710.50	(£14.10 × 405 units)
Contribution: 400 skateboards	5,640.00	(£14.10 × 400 units)
Contribution	**70.50**	

As a result of fixed costs remaining the same as activity (or output) changes, contribution and profit increase or decrease by the same amount.

Change in contribution = Change in profit

FURTHER EXAMPLE

Using the data from our first example, determine the contribution and profit if 370 skateboards had been made and sold in the period (revenue/unit, variable cost/unit and fixed costs remain as before).

Solution

	£	
Sales	7,400	(£20.00 × 370 units)
less Variable costs	(2,183)	(£5.90 × 370 units)
Contribution	5,217	
less Fixed costs	(3,340)	
Profit	**1,877**	

Alternatively, this may be solved as follows:

	£	
Profit for 400 skateboards	2,300	
less Contribution lost	(423)	(£14.10 × (400 − 370) 30 units)
Profit	**1,877**	

Contribution/sales ratio

The relationship between contribution and profit was discussed above. The relationship between contribution and sales is dealt with by the contribution to sales ratio (sometimes referred to as the profit volume ratio). The ratio is normally expressed as a percentage and is abbreviated to *C/S ratio*. It indicates the rate at which profit is earned.

$$\text{C/S ratio} = \frac{\text{Contribution}}{\text{Sales}} \times 100\%$$

EXAMPLE

Using the data from our skateboard example above, the contribution/sales ratio is

$$\text{C/S ratio} = \frac{5,640}{8,000} \times 100\% = 70.5\%$$

The proportion of sales revenue that remains as contribution is 70.5%. This percentage will remain constant whatever the level of output of skateboards, because there is a linear relationship between cost and output (or activity) and sales and output (or activity).

In our example if sales revenue increases by (say) one-third, then variable costs would also rise by the same proportion. The proportion of revenue that remains as contribution would, however, be constant at 70.5%.

Contribution/sales ratio application

The C/S ratio is particularly useful for what-if analysis, reflecting changes in output or activity and the associated cost implications, and also as a short-run decision-making technique where the best use of existing capacity must be made (the latter will be addressed in Chapter 9).

It is also beneficial for calculating the extra contribution from extra sales. Our earlier example required the extra contribution to be determined from the sale of a further 5 skateboards (at £20 each).

Using the C/S ratio already determined for this example (70.5%) the extra contribution would be:

(5 skateboards × £20) = £100 × 70.5% (C/S ratio) = **£70.50**

The answer is the same as our previous solution.

Breakeven (CVP) analysis

One of the most frequent applications of marginal costing is in the study of breakeven analysis. The breakeven point for an organisation is the point where neither a profit nor loss is incurred. This is the point where the contribution exactly equals the fixed costs. Such analysis provides useful information for management, for example how far sales may fall before a loss will be incurred by the business. Breakeven analysis could also provide information on the margin of safety of the organisation, i.e. the level (sales revenue or volume) above the breakeven point at which the business normally operates.

Breakeven analysis is frequently referred to as CVP (cost volume profit) analysis and is regularly used in what-if analysis and short-run decision making. CVP analysis studies the relationship between costs, volume of output or activity and profit. It is most relevant where the proposed changes in activity levels are relatively small, i.e. within the *relevant range of activity* for the business.

Typical short-run decisions where CVP analysis can prove to be beneficial are sales mix (where more than one product or service exists), pricing policy and special order acceptance. CVP analysis may be determined by graphical means or by formula.

Breakeven (CVP) analysis by formula

- Breakeven point (units): $\dfrac{\text{Fixed costs}}{\text{Contribution per unit}}$

- Breakeven point (revenue): $\dfrac{\text{Fixed costs}}{\text{C/S ratio}}$

- Sales level to achieve a target profit (units): $\dfrac{\text{Fixed costs} + \text{Target profit}}{\text{Contribution per unit}}$

- Sales level to achieve a target profit (revenue): $\dfrac{\text{Fixed costs} + \text{Target profit}}{\text{C/S ratio}}$

EXAMPLE

A company manufactures a product, which has a variable cost of £8 per unit and a selling price of £13 per unit. Fixed costs are £25,000. The target profit is £10,000.

Solution

- Breakeven point (units): $\dfrac{25,000}{5} = \textbf{5000 units}$

- Breakeven point (revenue): $\dfrac{25,000}{5/13} = \textbf{£65,000 units}$

- Sales level to achieve a target profit (units): $\dfrac{25{,}000 + 10{,}000}{5} = $ **7000 units**

- Sales level to achieve a target profit (revenue): $\dfrac{25{,}000 + 10{,}000}{5/13} = $ **£91,000**

Reconciliation of the breakeven point

The breakeven calculations may be proved using the marginal cost statement to determine the profit at 5000 units.

Sales	65,000	(£13.00 × 5000 units)
less Variable costs	(40,000)	(£8.00 × 5000 units)
Contribution	25,000	
less Fixed costs	(25,000)	
Profit/Loss	**nil**	

Margin of safety

We mentioned the term margin of safety in our introduction to breakeven analysis. The margin of safety represents a comparison between the budgeted level of sales expressed in £'s or units and the breakeven point of the organisation.

EXAMPLE

A company manufactures 4000 units of a product, which has a variable cost of £15 per unit and a selling price of £23 per unit. Fixed costs are £25,000. The target profit is £10,000.

Determine the breakeven point and margin of safety.

Solution

- Breakeven point (units): $\dfrac{25{,}000}{8} = $ **3125 units**

- Breakeven point (revenue): $\dfrac{25{,}000}{8/23} = $ **£71,875**

- Margin of safety: $4000 - 3125 = $ **875 units**

or

$$875 \text{ units} \times £23 = \textbf{£20,125}$$

This may also be expressed as a percentage:

$$\frac{875 \text{ units}}{4000 \text{ units}} = \textbf{21.875\%}$$

Breakeven charts

Breakeven charts are an alternative to using formulae to determine the breakeven point and margin of safety. This is advantageous where an overview free of detail is required.

The construction of a breakeven chart is best illustrated by an example.

EXAMPLE

Using the data from our margin of safety example above, construct a breakeven chart, showing the breakeven point, margin of safety and the profit.

Figure 16 was constructed using the following approach:

- **Appropriately scaled axis**   The x-axis shows level of activity expressed in units of output or activity. The y-axis shows cost and revenue values in £'s.
- **Fixed cost line**   A straight line that runs parallel with the x-axis (horizontal) and intersects the y-axis at the amount of the fixed costs (in this case £25,000). Fixed costs remain the same at all levels of activity (or output).

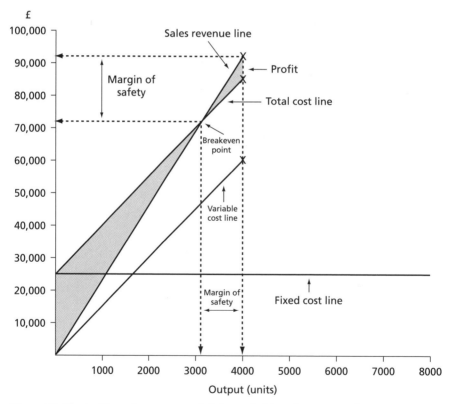

Figure 16 Illustration of an appropriately scaled breakeven graph

- **Variable cost line**   A straight line that cuts through the origin (0,0) and increases by the amount of the variable cost per unit. Only two sets of coordinates are required to draw a straight line on a graph, the first point being the origin; the second point should be at the normal level of activity (or output). The gradient of the line remains unchanged as the variable cost per unit is constant at all activity (or output) levels.

    For example, the total variable cost at the output level of 4000 units is

    £15 × 4000 units = £60,000

Therefore the second coordinate should be (4000, 60,000).

- **Sales revenue line**   A straight line that cuts through the origin (0,0) and increases by the amount of the selling price per unit. Again only two sets of coordinates are required, the first point being the origin, the second point being at the normal level of activity (or output). The gradient of the line remains unchanged since the selling price per unit is constant at all activity (or output) levels.

    For example, the total sales revenue at the output level of 4000 units is

    £23 × 4000 units = £92,000

Therefore the second coordinate should be (4000, 92,000).

- **Total cost line**   Variable costs are added to the fixed costs to derive a total cost line. The total cost line commences at the point where the fixed cost line intersects the y-axis, in this case coordinate (0, 25,000) and will appear parallel to the variable cost line. The second coordinate should be at the normal level of activity (or output).

    For example, the total cost at the output level of 4000 units is

Variable cost: £15 × 4000 units	=	£60,000
Fixed cost	=	£25,000
Total cost		£85,000

Therefore the second coordinate should be (4000, 85,000).

The breakeven point may be determined from the graph where the total revenue line intersects the total cost line. This is the point where total revenue equals total cost and the organisation breaks even.

Figure 16 confirms the breakeven data provided by the formulae in our solution above as follows:

- Breakeven point (units): **3125 units**

- Breakeven point (revenue): **£71,875**

- Margin of safety: **875 units** *or* **£20,125**

Profit volume charts

A profit volume chart is an alternative form of presentation. It emphasises the change of profit at different activity levels. In this case, lines for sales, variable costs and fixed costs are not included. For this chart only a single line is drawn.

The construction of a profit volume chart is again best illustrated by an example.

EXAMPLE

Using the same data as above, construct a profit volume chart, showing the breakeven point, margin of safety and the profit.

Figure 17 was constructed using the following approach:

- **Appropriately scaled axis** The x-axis shows level of sales expressed in units of output or revenue (£'s). The y-axis shows profit and loss values in £'s.
- **Contribution line** This single line shows profit/loss at different activity (or output) levels. The line commences at the point equal to the fixed costs at zero output, in this case coordinate $(0, -25,000)$ since there will be a loss of £25,000 as the fixed costs will still be incurred at zero output. The second coordinate should be at the normal level of activity (or output).

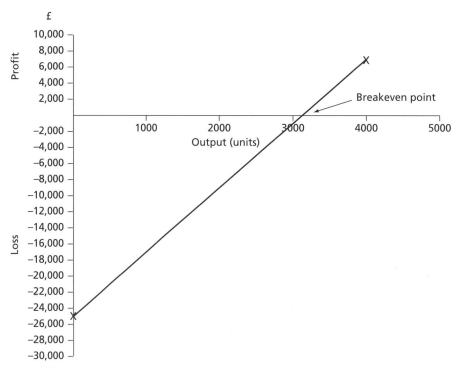

Figure 17 Illustration of an appropriately scaled profit volume chart

For example the profit at the output level of 4000 units is

	£
Sales revenue: £23 × 4,000 units	92,000
Variable cost: £15 × 4,000 units	(60,000)
Contribution	32,000
Fixed cost	(25,000)
Profit	7,000

Therefore the second coordinate should be (4000, 7000).

The breakeven point may be determined from the graph where this single line intercepts the x-axis.

Figure 17 confirms the breakeven data provided by the formulae in the solution to our margin of safety example and in Figure 16 as follows:

- Breakeven point (units): **3125 units**
- Breakeven point (revenue): **£71,875** (3,125 × £23)
- Margin of safety: **875 units** or **£20,125**
- *Profit* may also be determined from the graph as **£7,000**.

Assumptions and limitations of breakeven analysis

Breakeven analysis is a valuable, widely used short-term decision-making technique. However, it does have limitations and any solution must be interpreted with care.

The major assumptions of the analysis are:

- Fixed costs remain the same regardless of changes in activity levels.
- The variable cost per unit remains constant for all levels of activity.
- The selling price per unit will remain constant at all activity (or output) levels.

  (The above assumptions are likely to be valid within the *relevant range* of activity, and within this range, cost estimates are likely to hold good.)

- Stock levels remain the same. Items are not produced for stock, but sold immediately. Therefore sales revenue and variable costs are for the same activity (or output) levels.
- Estimates of fixed costs, variable costs and selling prices are known at the outset with certainty.

Provided that any solution is interpreted in the light of the above limitations, breakeven or CVP analysis is a valuable aid to management for short-term decision making and what-if analysis. The graphical illustrations in Figures 16 and 17 provide a useful overview.

Marginal costing vs. absorption (full) costing

Marginal costing may also be utilised as an alternative to absorption costing for the calculation of costs and the valuation of stocks for the purpose of profit determination.

Absorption costing allows all costs to be absorbed into units of output or activity, irrespective of whether the cost is fixed or variable. The mechanisms to accommodate this were discussed in Chapter 6. The calculation of costs and valuation of stocks contains both fixed and variable cost elements.

Marginal costing allows only the variable costs to be included into units of output or activity. Therefore the calculation of costs and valuation of stocks contains only variable cost elements. Fixed costs are deducted in total and no attempt is made to absorb these costs into output or activity.

Marginal and absorption costing treat overhead in a different manner, the latter incorporating the overhead into the product or service and the former excluding the overhead from the product or service, instead deducting it in total at the end of the period. This may result in different product or service profitability and different stock valuations, depending on the method used.

The two approaches are contrasted in the following example.

EXAMPLE

Period 1

Opening stock	nil
Sales volume	10,000 units
Selling price	£5/unit
Production	15,000 units

Production costs:	£
Direct material	15,000
Direct labour	30,000
Variable expenses	6,000
Fixed expenses	12,000
	63,000

Period 2

Opening stock	5000 units
Sales volume	15,000 units
Selling price	£5/unit
Production	10,000 units

Production costs:

Unit variable costs   as per period 1
Fixed expenses   £12,000

Prepare profit statements based on both marginal costing and absorption costing techniques for periods 1 and 2.

Solution

Workings

	£/unit	
Direct material	1.0	(£15,000/15,000 units)
Direct labour	2.0	(£30,000/15,000 units)
Variable expenses	0.4	(£6000/15,000 units)
Total variable cost	3.4	
Fixed costs	0.8	(£12,000/15,000 units)
Full cost	4.2	

Period 1

	Absorption costing		Marginal costing	
	£'000s	£'000s	£'000s	£'000s
Sales		50		50
Opening stock	nil		nil	
Production cost:				
Direct material	15		15	
Direct labour	30		30	
Variable expenses	6		6	
Fixed costs	12		–	
	63		51	
Closing stock	(21)[1]		(17)[2]	
Cost of sales		(42)		(34)
Contribution		–		16
Fixed costs		–		(12)
Profit		8		4

[1] 5000 units × £4.20 (full cost)
[2] 5000 units × £3.40 (variable cost)

The profit for period 1 using an absorption costing approach is £8000 whereas the profit for the same period using a marginal costing approach is £4000.

Period 2

	Absorption costing		Marginal costing	
	£'000s	£'000s	£'000s	£'000s
Sales		75		75
Opening stock	21[(1)]		17[(2)]	
Production cost:				
Direct material	10		10	
Direct labour	20		20	
Variable expenses	4		4	
Fixed costs	12		–	
	46		34	
Closing stock	nil		nil	
Cost of sales		(67)		(51)
Contribution		–		24
Fixed costs		–		(12)
Profit		8		12

[(1)] 5000 units × £4.20 (full cost)
[(2)] 5000 units × £3.40 (variable cost)

The profit for period 2 using an absorption costing approach is £8000 whereas the profit for the same period using a marginal costing approach is now £12,000.

Profit summary

	Absorption costing		Marginal costing
	£'000s		£'000s
Period 1	8		4
Period 2	8		12
Total	16	←Same →	16

Discussion

The difference in profit figures is caused by the dissimilar treatment of fixed costs under the two methods of costing when valuing stock. With marginal costing, the fixed costs are written off as period costs and stock is valued at variable cost, as opposed to full cost under absorption costing. The inclusion of fixed costs in stock valuation transfers some of the period's fixed costs into the next period. As a result of the two methods differing in their valuation of stock, they produce different profit figures when stocks arise.

The difference in profit in our example arises because fixed costs of £4000 are charged into period 2 under absorption costing, whereas under marginal costing this was written off in period 1, depressing profits by the same amount.

Difference in profit:

5000 (stock) units × £0.80 (fixed costs per unit) = £4000

Both marginal and absorption costing produce the same profit where there are no stock changes. In our example there is no stock at the beginning of period 1 and none at the end of period 2. It follows that aggregate profit for both periods is the same.

Which technique should be used?

The technique that is most appropriate for a particular organisation should be used. However, the following observations should be borne in mind when making the choice:

- Marginal costing does not require complex apportionments.
- Fixed costs are incurred on a time basis. It therefore appears prudent to write off these costs in the same manner.
- Marginal costing profit statements may be more useful for decision making.
- Statutory valuations of stock require that fixed costs are included in stock units, thereby favouring absorption costing.
- The inclusion of fixed costs in stock valuation allows the matching of the expense with the revenue when the stock is sold, thereby smoothing out profits between periods.

Summary

- Marginal costing may be used for.
  - the determination of costs for products or services,
  - the calculation of breakeven points,
  - what-if analysis, reflecting changes in output or activity,
  - as a short-run decision-making technique.

- Marginal costing is the principle whereby:
  - only variable costs are charged to units of output or activity,
  - fixed costs are written off in full against the contribution for the period.

- Marginal costing treats overhead as a period cost.

- Absorption costing attempts to unitise overhead into the cost of the product or service.

- The use of contribution is helpful for decision making, as it excludes fixed costs.
  - The change in contribution will equal the change in profit.

- The relationship between contribution and sales is dealt with by the C/S ratio.
  - This indicates the rate at which profit is earned from sales.

- Breakeven (CVP) analysis may be carried out by graphical means or by formulae. The following may be determined:
  - breakeven point (units),
  - breakeven point (revenue),
  - margin of safety.

- Breakeven (CVP) analysis by graphical means may be determined by:
  - a breakeven chart,
  - a profit volume chart.

- The assumptions and limitations of breakeven analysis are:
  - Fixed costs remain constant.
  - Variable costs per unit remain constant.
  - Selling price per unit remains constant.
  - Stock levels remain unchanged.
  - Estimates of costs and selling prices are known with certainty.

- Marginal and absorption costing techniques will result in different profit figures where there are changes in stock levels.
  - The inclusion of fixed costs in stock valuation (under absorption costing) transfers some of the fixed costs to the following period.

Questions for review

1 Define marginal cost and give an example to illustrate this.

2 Define contribution and give a numerical example to illustrate this.

3 Illustrate with the aid of a breakeven graph the breakeven point.

4 Illustrate with the aid of a breakeven graph the margin of safety.

5 Illustrate with the aid of a profit volume graph the breakeven point.

6 Illustrate with the aid of a profit volume graph the area of profit and loss.

7 Prepare a revenue statement in a marginal costing format.

8 What is the significance of the C/S ratio where extra sales are made?

9 Determine the following CVP analysis formulae:

   a Breakeven point (units)
   b Breakeven point (revenue)
   c Sales level to achieve a target profit (units)
   d Sales level to achieve a target profit (revenue)

10 Give *three* examples of situations where CVP analysis could prove useful.

11 Discuss the reasons for the difference in profits recorded under marginal costing and absorption costing where there are changes in stock levels.

12 Demonstrate with the aid of a profit statement how the valuation of closing stock under absorption costing, transfers fixed costs to the following period.

Self-assessment questions

(*Denotes that a suggested solution may be found at the end of this book.)

1* Breakeven point and margin of safety calculation

A company manufactures 8000 units of a product, which has a variable cost of £15 per unit and a selling price of £20 per unit. Fixed costs are £25,000. The target profit is £10,000.

   Determine the breakeven point and margin of safety.

2* Profit determination

The following data was extracted from the accounts of a bed manufacturer:

	Total cost (£)	Fixed cost (£)	Variable cost (£)
Direct labour	1800	1500	300
Direct material	2200	–	2200
Overhead	1900	1840	60
	5900	3340	2560

   a If 40 beds are manufactured and sold for £200 each in the period, determine the profit in a marginal costing format.
   b Determine the contribution and profit if 37 beds are made and sold in the period (revenue/unit, variable cost/unit and fixed costs remain as before).

3 Breakeven chart

From the following data construct a breakeven chart and determine:

   a The breakeven point
   b The profit

	£
Fixed cost	40,000
Variable cost	60,000
Sales	120,000
Output (units)	120,000

4 Profit volume chart

Construct a profit volume chart from the following data:

Sales	£8/unit
Variable cost	£5/unit
Fixed cost	£15,000
Output (units)	7000

5 Limitations of breakeven analysis

Discuss the underlying assumptions and limitations of breakeven analysis and whether they invalidate the technique.

6* Comparison of profit statements using marginal costing and absorption costing

Prepare profit statements based on both marginal costing and absorption costing techniques for periods 1 and 2 from the following data:

Period 1

Opening stock	nil
Sales volume	10,000 units
Selling price	£5/unit
Production	12,000 units

Production costs:	£
Direct material	15,000
Direct labour	12,000
Variable expenses	6,000
Fixed expenses	12,000
	45,000

Period 2

Opening stock	2,000 units
Sales volume	12,000 units
Selling price	£5/unit
Production	10,000 units

Production costs:	
Unit variable costs	as per period 1
Fixed expenses	£12,000

7* Breakeven point calculation using formulae and determination using charts

A company has production facilities that may be used to manufacture 80,000 units during the period. Each unit is sold for £5, the variable cost of production is £4, and fixed factory overheads are £50,000.

a Determine the breakeven point in units and sales value using formulae.
b Calculate the margin of safety as a percentage.
c Construct a breakeven chart, clearly indicating the breakeven point.
d Construct a profit volume chart, clearly indicating the areas of profit and loss.

Chapter 9

Marginal costing short-term decision making

Chapter objectives

Having studied this chapter you should be able to:

- understand the significance of contribution in short-term decision making;
- understand how marginal costing may be utilised in short-term decision making;
- explain the term key factor (or principal factor);
- be able to demonstrate the application of marginal costing to the following short-run decision-making problems: make or buy, acceptance of a one off order, discontinuing a product, choice of a product where a shortage exists;
- explain the term opportunity cost;
- appreciate the limitations of marginal costing in short-term decision making.

Introduction

Decision making involves a choice between alternatives and inevitably relates to a future period. For this reason, only future costs and revenues are of interest to the decision maker. Past costs may prove useful, but only in so far as they provide a guide to the future. In making a short-run, tactical business decision there are many factors that may have to be considered. Profitability may be paramount, but there are other considerations relating to existing customers, working capital, quality, overall impact on the organisation and so on.

The purpose of this chapter is to continue the study of marginal costing to provide an appreciation of the different types of decision where marginal costing may prove beneficial, specifically in the context of short-term decision making, where the best use of existing capacity must be made. In utilising only existing capacity, fixed costs remain unchanged in the short term and decisions may be made on the basis of contribution rather than profit, as the latter would include fixed costs.

Marginal costing is particularly appropriate for short-term decision making as the concept of contribution enables only those costs and revenues that change as a result of a particular course of action to be considered. Contribution allows the viability of a product or service to be determined without the additional complexity of fixed costs being introduced into an individual product line or service. Instead fixed costs may be written off against total contribution to determine overall profitability.

Marginal costing may be used for the following types of short-run decisions:

- make or buy,
- acceptance of a one off order,
- discontinuing a product,
- choice of a product where a shortage exists.

What is short-term decision making?

Short-term decision making relates to the future, where a choice exists between alternatives, and the best use of existing capacity must be made. As mentioned above, in utilising existing capacity only, fixed costs remain unchanged in the short term, so decisions may be made on the basis of contribution rather than profit. It is therefore appropriate to utilise marginal costing for such decision making as only variable costs are charged to units of production or service. The fixed cost or overhead relating to the period where the production or service took place is written off in full against the contribution of that period.

Short-run decisions

We identified above four distinct decisions where marginal costing can prove useful for decision makers and we shall now discuss these in more detail.

Make or buy

This refers to the situation where a product could be made in-house or bought in from a supplier. There are a variety of technical considerations that may be taken into account in reaching the decision (which are outside the scope of this text). Cost will be of overriding importance and marginal costing can prove useful in enabling a comparison to be made between the cost of buying in the product and the marginal cost of manufacture. Fixed costs are excluded from the analysis, as they would be incurred in any case. However, should the fixed costs be incremental with regard to the decision, they would be included in determining profit.

EXAMPLE

The following data relates to a company manufacturing modems:

Production/sales	50,000 units
Fixed costs	£400,000
	£/unit
Material	15.50
Labour	17.50
Variable overhead	21.00
Marginal cost of manufacture	**54.00**
Fixed costs/unit	8.00 (£400,000/50,000 units)
Total product cost	62.00

An external supplier has offered to supply the modems at **£59.50/unit**. The production capacity of the company would not be used elsewhere if it were not employed in the manufacture of modems.

Should the company make or buy the modems?

Solution

A comparison should be made between the marginal cost of manufacture of the modems and the cost of buying in. The fixed costs of £400,000 would be incurred irrespective of whether the modems are manufactured or bought in.

	£/unit
Marginal cost of manufacture	54.00
Cost of buying in	59.50
Benefit of manufacture	**5.50**

The company should make, rather than buy the modems.

Proof

	Manufactured (£000's)	Bought in (£000's)
Purchase		2,975
Material	775	
Labour	875	
Variable overhead	1,050	
Fixed costs	400	400
Total cost	3,100	3,375

If the modems are bought in, the total cost will increase by £3,375,000 − £3,100,000 = £275,000 (or £5.50 × 50,000 units). Overall profits would therefore fall by the same amount.

Acceptance of a one off order

This refers to the situation where normal production would remain unaffected and spare capacity exists so as to facilitate a one off order, usually at a lower than normal price, without causing disruption to the regular production. There are a variety of technical and marketing considerations that may be taken into account in reaching a decision whether to accept a special order or decline it, not least the reaction of regular customers to a similar product being offered to another customer at a reduced price. Cost again will be of paramount importance in reaching such a decision and marginal costing can prove useful in enabling a decision to be reached. Fixed costs are excluded from the analysis, as they would be incurred in any case. However, should the fixed costs be incremental with regard to the one off order, they would be included in determining profit.

EXAMPLE

The following data relates to a company manufacturing keyboards for computers:

Production/sales	10,000 units
Fixed costs	£75,000

	£/unit
Selling price	15.00
Material	2.50
Labour	1.50
Variable overhead	3.00
Marginal cost of manufacture	7.00

A new customer is prepared to buy an additional 3000 keyboards, provided the price is only £9 each. The factory has spare capacity to undertake this order without the need to disrupt regular production The order would be packaged as an 'own brand product' so as to differentiate it from the keyboards supplied to existing customers.

Should the company accept the additional order?

Solution

As the firm has spare manufacturing capacity and regular production would be unaffected, then the order could be accepted as the selling price of £9/unit is greater than the marginal cost of £7/unit. Fixed costs will remain unchanged, as there is spare capacity. Additional contribution of (£9 − £7) × 3000 units = £6000 will be generated and overall profit will increase by the same amount.

Proof

	Original (£000's)	Original and one off order (£000's)
Sales revenue	150	177
Variable costs	(70)	(91)
Contribution	80	86
Fixed costs	(75)	(75)
Profit	5	11

Profit would increase by £11,000 − £5000 = £6000. On purely financial grounds, the special order should be accepted.

The following non-financial factors could also be taken into consideration.

● If the order were accepted, what would the reaction be of existing customers?

● Can the spare capacity be used for other, more profitable work now?

● Would the spare capacity be used for more profitable work later, when the special order may still be being completed?

● Would such a large order, at a significantly lower price, lead to a change in pricing policy of all companies in the market?

Discontinuing a product

This refers to the situation where a company produces several products, one or more of which may not be considered viable on the basis of profitability. In such circumstances, consideration should be given to discontinuing the unprofitable product(s) from the product range. As in the earlier examples, there may be a variety of technical considerations (outside the scope of this text) that may be taken into account in reaching the decision, including sales interdependency of product lines, for example nuts and bolts.

Marginal costing can prove useful to evaluate the contribution per product. In the analysis of a problem of this type it must be borne in mind that if a product is discontinued, the variable costs will no longer be incurred, but the fixed costs for the business as a whole are likely to remain unchanged. Therefore fixed costs of any discontinued product will have to be borne by the remaining products. Under these circumstances, any product with a positive contribution should be continued, as some contribution will be generated to go towards paying for fixed costs in total.

EXAMPLE

The following data relates to a company manufacturing four products:

Product	1	2	3	4
	£'000s	£'000s	£'000s	£'000s
Sales	550	750	200	260
Variable costs	330	550	100	160
Fixed costs	100	75	125	110
Profit/(loss)	120	125	(25)	(10)

It has been suggested that products 3 and 4 be discontinued from production as they are both loss making.

Based upon the above data, should products 3 and 4 be discontinued?

Solution

Product	1	2	3	4
	£'000s	£'000s	£'000s	£'000s
Sales	550	750	200	260
Variable costs	(330)	(550)	(100)	(160)
Contribution	**220**	**200**	**100**	**100**

All products make a positive contribution and should therefore be continued.

If products 3 and 4 were discontinued the effects on profits would be as follows.

Original production plan

	£000's	
Contribution product 1	220	
Contribution product 2	200	
Contribution product 3	100	
Contribution product 4	100	
Total contribution	620	
less Fixed costs	410	(100 + 75 + 125 + 110)
Profit	210	

Revised production plan (discontinuing products 3 and 4)

	£000's
Contribution product 1	220
Contribution product 2	200
Total contribution	420
less Fixed costs	410 (100 + 75 + 125 + 110)
Profit	10

If products 3 and 4 were discontinued, profit would be reduced to £10,000. The reduction in profit of £210,000 − £10,000 = £200,000 is the same as the lost contribution of £100,000 + £100,000 = £200,000 that would occur as a result of discontinuing products 3 and 4.

Choice of a product where a shortage exists

This refers to the situation where a company produces several products, but there is a shortage or single binding constraint. Such a constraint prohibits further profits being made, and may be, for example, sales, availability of skilled labour or availability of materials that may be in short supply.

In such circumstances, consideration should be given to maximising the contribution per unit of scarce resource consumed. As in the earlier examples, there may be a variety of technical considerations (again outside the scope of this text) that may be taken into account in ranking products where a shortage exists, including sales interdependency of product lines.

Marginal costing can, however, prove useful to evaluate the contribution per unit of scarce resource or limiting factor. This may be used as the basis to determine a production plan, based upon the availability of scarce resources and maximum demand. The contribution per limiting factor (or key factor) should be maximised as this will in turn maximise the contribution and hence the profit of the business as a whole.

The following points should be borne in mind when applying limiting factor analysis:

- Fixed costs will remain the same irrespective of the production plan. Therefore profit maximisation and contribution maximising outputs are the same.

- Units of output are divisible and a profit maximising solution may accordingly include fractions of units as the optimum output. Fractional solutions may not be feasible.

- The practice of maximising the contribution per unit of scarce resource is only suitable where there is a single binding constraint. If there are many constraints, this technique is unsuitable. In this situation the resource allocation model of linear programming should be utilised.

EXAMPLE

The following unit data relates to a company manufacturing four products:

Product	1	2	3	4
Maximum demand (units)	1,000	1,550	1,250	1,375
	£	£	£	£
Sales	30	54	20	25
Variable costs				
Material	10	20	6	8
Labour	12	24	5	12
Contribution	8	10	9	5

All four products are produced using the same material that costs £2 per kg and is currently in short supply. Due to the supply difficulties only 21,750 kg is available for the period in question. Fixed costs amount to £12,000 for this period.

Determine the optimal production plan, assuming that the company wishes to maximise profits.

Solution

All four products have a positive contribution. If there were no shortage of materials, the production plan would be the maximum demand for the products. However, given that materials are limited to 21,750 kg, contribution per kg of material (key factor or limiting factor) must be determined and the products ranked in order of preference for production.

Contribution per key factor

Product	1	2	3	4
Contribution	8	10	9	5
Material/unit	5	10	3	4
Contribution per unit of material	1.6	1	3	1.25
Ranking	2	4	1	3

The contribution per key factor (in this case per unit of material) shows the amount of contribution produced per unit of scarce resource consumed (in this case kg of material).

Production plan

1,250 units of product 3, consuming	3,750 kg
1,000 units of product 1, consuming	5,000 kg
1,375 units of product 4, consuming	5,500 kg
750 units of product 2, consuming	7,500 kg
	21,750 kg

We can confirm that the production schedule determined is optimum, by comparing the profit generated using the above schedule with a production schedule based upon ranking of contribution only (i.e. a production plan based upon contribution per unit only).

Profit generated using contribution per key factor:

Product	1	2	3	4	Total
Production plan (units)	1,000	750	1,250	1,375	
	£	£	£	£	£
Contribution	8,000	7,500	11,250	6,875	33,625
Fixed costs					(12,000)
Profit					21,625

Production plan using ranking of contribution only (as opposed to contribution per key factor):

Production plan

1,550 units of product 2, consuming	15,500 kg
1,250 units of product 3, consuming	3,750 kg
500 units of product 1, consuming	2,500 kg
0 units of product 4, consuming	0 kg
	21,750 kg

Profit generated using ranking of contribution only:

Product	1	2	3	4	Total
Production plan (units)	500	1,550	1,250	0	
	£	£	£	£	£
Contribution	4,000	15,500	11,250		30,750
Fixed costs					(12,000)
Profit					18,750

The profit generated using contribution per limiting factor (or key factor) is £21,625 − £18,750 = £2,875 higher than using ranking of contribution only.

Summary

- Decision making relates to the future and is a choice between alternatives.
  - Information for decision making is based upon data for future costs and revenues that will change as a result of the decision.
- Marginal costing may be used in a variety of decision-making situations including:
  - make or buy,
  - acceptance of a one off order,
  - discontinuing a product,
  - choice of a product where a shortage exists.
- In decision-making situations, there may be a variety of considerations taken into account, other than cost or profitability. Such considerations may include:
  - sales interdependency of product lines,
  - working capital,
  - quality,
  - reaction of existing customers,
  - production changes as a result of the decision.
- Marginal costing is most appropriate for short-run decisions, where fixed costs do not change as a consequence of the decision taken.
  - Should fixed costs be incremental with regard to the decision, they should be included in determining profit.

Questions for review

1 Define short-term decision making and give an example to illustrate this.

2 Give *three* examples of situations where marginal costing for decision making could prove useful.

3 Define key factor (or limiting factor) and give a numerical example to illustrate this.

4 Illustrate how marginal costing may be used in a make or buy decision.

5 Illustrate how marginal costing may be used in an acceptance of a one off order decision.

6 Illustrate how marginal costing may be used in a discontinuing of a product decision.

7 Illustrate how marginal costing may be used in ranking of products where a single binding constraint exists.

8 Discuss the reason for short-run decision making emphasising contribution rather than profit.

9 Discuss how incremental fixed costs may be incorporated into your analysis, for decision-making purposes.

10 Describe the steps you would take to identify if a shortage of a key factor exists.

11 Explain the significance of a firm having spare capacity when considering whether to accept a one off order.

Self-assessment questions

(*Denotes that a suggested solution may be found at the end of this book.)

1* Make or buy

A company manufactures a wide range of electrical products, one of which is a compact transistor, with a variable cost of £15 per unit and a selling price of £20 per unit. In each period 8000 units are made and sold. Fixed costs are £25,000. An external company has offered to supply all of the transistors to the company at a cost of £18 per unit.

Determine whether the company should make or buy the transistors.

2* One off order

The following data was extracted from the accounts of a clock manufacturer:

	£/unit	£ total
Sales	15	150,000
Fixed costs		70,000
Variable costs	7	

The firm currently has spare capacity and has been approached by a Malaysian customer to supply a one off order of an additional 2500 clocks at a lower price of £8/unit.

a Determine whether the clock manufacturer should accept the one off order.

b Comment on the wider commercial considerations arising from such a decision.

3* Discontinuing a product

The following data relates to a company manufacturing four products:

Product	1	2	3	4
	£'000s	£'000s	£'000s	£'000s
Sales	550	750	200	260
Variable costs	330	600	100	360
Fixed costs	100	55	125	50
Profit/(loss)	120	95	(25)	(150)

It has been suggested that products 3 and 4 be discontinued from production as they are both loss making.

a Based upon the above data, should products 3 and 4 be discontinued?

b Determine the overall profitability if your recommendations in question (a) are implemented. Compare this with the overall profitability of the original production plan and comment on your findings.

4* Choice of product where a shortage exists

The following unit data relates to a company manufacturing four products:

Product	1	2	3	4
Maximum demand (units)	1,000	1,550	1,250	1,375
	£	£	£	£
Sales	30	54	20	25
Variable costs				
Material	10	20	6	8
Labour	12	24	5	12
Contribution	8	10	9	5

All four products are produced using the same material that costs £4 per kg and is currently in short supply. Due to the supply difficulties only 10,000 kg is available for the period in question. Fixed costs amount to £12,000 for the period.

a Determine the optimal production plan, assuming that the company wishes to maximise profits.

b Confirm the production schedule is optimum, by comparing the profit generated in your answer to question (a) above with a production schedule based upon ranking of contribution only.

Chapter 10

Planning and budgeting

Chapter objectives

Having studied this chapter you should be able to:

- explain the meaning of the term budget;
- understand the importance of the budgetary process;
- demonstrate the interrelationship of budgets;
- discuss the human behavioural aspects of budgeting;
- discuss the advantages and disadvantages of budgeting;
- explain the principles of zero based budgeting;
- understand how activity based budgeting may be applied.

Introduction

The purpose of this chapter is to introduce planning and budgeting. It is vital that every organisation has some form of plan in order that management and employees all work towards the same goals. Once plans have been agreed and put in place, the organisation may monitor and control its activities by comparing what actually occurs with what was planned for. In this way where a significant deviation from plans occurs, corrective action may be taken by management to get the business back on course to achieve its objectives.

A budget is a plan of action expressed in financial terms. It is this quantification of plans which sets budgeting apart from the other types of planning which may go on in an organisation. The vast majority of businesses prepare some sort of budget in advance of a period of time (often one year) that is referred to as the budget period. Budgets may be prepared in summary format or may be quite detailed for each business function, for example, sales, administration etc. The type of budgets prepared and level of detail found in them will vary between organisations.

Once budgets are prepared, the financial data may be communicated to appropriate personnel who are responsible for achieving specific goals. For example, details of the sales budget may be passed to the sales manager in order that he or she may be aware of the level of sales required for each product.

In this chapter we will discuss the preparation of budgets and their benefits and motivational aspects, and examples will be given of the major types of budgets and how they may interrelate for the benefit of an organisation. Alternative budgeting approaches will also be discussed in an attempt to address the limitations of traditional budgetary systems.

What is a budget?

A budget is a plan of action expressed in financial terms relating to a future period. Ideally, it should encompass all of the activities of the business and should involve personnel throughout the organisation in its preparation. The preparation of budgets is not something that can be carried out by accountants alone. It requires the participation of many managers and other personnel to ensure that the plans for the forthcoming period are translated into a realistic and feasible financial plan, which all employees will strive to achieve.

From a behavioural point of view, an optimum budget is one which ensures that the goals of staff coincide with the goals of the organisation (*goal congruence*). For example, if sales targets are achieved, performance bonuses are paid to employees. It is therefore paramount not to impose budgets on staff, but to allow them to participate in the process of establishing targets. This is likely to increase motivation and encourage staff to work to achieve budgeted aims.

The preparation of a budget for an organisation will as a consequence facilitate:

- planning
- coordination
- motivation
- communication throughout the organisation
- control.

The organisational framework

The budget for any enterprise must operate within the organisational framework. If a budget is to succeed from a planning and control point of view, it must overlay the organisation's structure to ensure that responsibility and authority can be assigned to individual managers for achieving specific functional budgets. Individual managers may then delegate specific parts of their budgets to subordinates and only intervene if that part of the budget is not proceeding according to plan (i.e. manage the budget by exception).

Given the involvement of managers and their subordinates in implementing a budget, it is important that they are motivated and committed to achieving it.

Staff are likely to be more enthused if they have had the opportunity to participate in the budgetary process, rather than have the outcome forced upon them.

The budget framework

A budget should be prepared for a particular period of time identified at the outset. This is referred to as the *budget period*. A budget would be prepared from a long-range forecast or *strategic plan*, which an organisation may have for (say) the next five years. A strategic plan is likely to be very general in nature and contain very little detail, but would contain the overall objectives of the organisation. This plan would be broken down into shorter periods of time typically of one year, further subdivided into months.

Top management would develop an overall financial plan for the organisation for the year. This is termed the *master budget*. From this budget individual budgets are determined to represent functions or departments within the organisation. Budgets are hierarchical: as each part of the organisation should contribute to achieving overall corporate objectives each subordinate budget should also contribute to the master budget.

Integrated budgets

Each part of the business should not prepare its budgets in isolation or without reference to the overall master budget. For example, if the sales department plans to sell 30,000 cushions, 26,000 curtain sets and 10,000 rugs, the production department will be required to manufacture a similar number of these items (although a quantity of each may be held in stock which could be used). As a consequence of the decision to sell certain quantities and hence produce similar quantities, raw material quantities and labour requirements may then be determined. Once manufacturing requirements are known, estimates for the level of overhead to be incurred may be made. Consideration may then be given to selling and distribution costs, administration costs and the likely period of time before customers settle their debts.

Consideration may also be given as to whether new plant and equipment may need to be purchased and the credit period to be taken by the company before it settles its debts to suppliers.

The purpose of integrating budgets is to ensure that individual department's activities are properly coordinated and that the organisation will have sufficient funds available to meet its obligations as they fall due. In practice this is a complex and time-consuming exercise involving a considerable number of staff. The problem is made more difficult if the organisation is large or geographically dispersed. In order to coordinate the process a *budget committee* is often appointed to oversee the entire process (see below).

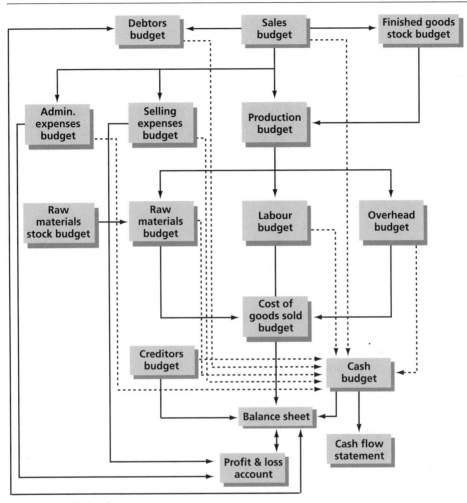

Figure 18 The budgetary process

The culmination of this exercise is a budgeted performance statement (the master budget) which reconciles the firm's overall budgeted position with the individual functional budgets. This performance statement is not dissimilar to a profit and loss account and balance sheet on a month-by-month basis. (A detailed discussion of the profit and loss account and balance sheet is beyond the scope of this text.)

Figure 18 illustrates the budgetary process.

Budget committee

Such is the importance of budgeting in organisations that a budget committee may be established to oversee the whole process. This is usually a high level steering committee that would attempt to:

- evaluate budgets produced to ensure that the organisations long-term objectives will be achieved;
- establish the roles and responsibilities of all participants in the process;
- establish the titles, responsibility and authority of all budget holders;
- confirm what budgets will be produced and in what order;
- develop a timetable for budget preparation;
- ensure that employees participate in the process;
- communicate the financial data to personnel.

Constructing an integrated budget

An integrated budget for a particular organisation will depend upon many specific factors relating to the business, including size of the business, nature of the activities carried out, departments, functions and possibly geographical locations. However, for the vast majority of businesses the sales budget is the starting point. Sales may refer to an operation in a hospital, for example, or cleaning a street for a local authority. An example of a sales budget and the major functional budgets of production and purchasing are shown below.

EXAMPLE – sales budget

The sales budget will involve the determination of the quantity of each product to be sold and the price per unit.

A company manufactures three types of product A, D and G. It is anticipated that sales quantities are likely to be 3000 units 4000 units and 5000 units respectively. The selling price has been agreed at £60, £70 and £80 respectively.
  Determine the sales budget.

Solution

	Quantity units	Price (£)	Sales value (£)
Product A	3,000	60	180,000
Product D	4,000	70	280,000
Product G	5,000	80	400,000
Total sales			860,000

EXAMPLE – production budget

The production budget will rely on the sales budget to determine the quantity of each product to be produced after taking into account stock holding policy.

Using the data above, determine the production budget assuming that the opening stocks of product A, D and G are 1000 units, 500 units and 750 units respectively and the company plans a 10% increase in finished goods stock at the end of the period.

Solution

Product	A	D	G
Sales forecast	3,000	4,000	5,000
+ Closing stock	1,100	550	825
	4,100	4,550	5,825
– Opening stock	(1,000)	(500)	(750)
Production	**3,100**	**4,050**	**5,075**

EXAMPLE – material (usage) budget

The material usage budget will require data from the production budget to determine the quantity of each product to be produced and the materials that will be consumed after taking into account stock holding policy for materials.

Using this information and the data from the production budget example, determine the material usage budget assuming that products A, D and G use materials alpha and beta as part of the manufacturing process. The opening stock levels for alpha and beta are 500 units and 1000 units respectively and the company plans to increase the closing stocks to 2000 units of alpha and 1750 units of beta. The materials used in manufacture are as follows:

	Alpha	Beta
Quantity/unit:		
Product A	5	2
Product D	2	1
Product G	2	3

Solution

	Alpha	Beta
Quantity used:		
Product A	15,500	6,200
(W1)		
Product D	8,100	4,050
(W2)		
Product G	10,150	15,225
(W3)		
Sub-total	33,750	25,475
+ Closing stock	2,000	1,750
− Opening stock	(500)	(1,000)
Usage quantity	35,250	26,225

Workings

(W1) Product A production $\times$ alpha quantity used $(3100 \times 5) = 15,500$
Product A production $\times$ beta quantity used $(3100 \times 2) = 6,200$

(W2) Product D production $\times$ alpha quantity used $(4050 \times 2) = 8,100$
Product D production $\times$ beta quantity used $(4050 \times 1) = 4,050$

(W3) Product G production $\times$ alpha quantity used $(5075 \times 2) = 10,150$
Product G production $\times$ beta quantity used $(5075 \times 3) = 15,225$

EXAMPLE – material (purchase) budget

The material purchase budget will be based upon the material usage budget including the price per unit for material to determine total material cost.

Using the data from the material usage budget example, determine the material purchase budget assuming that the unit cost of alpha and beta is £2 and £3 respectively.

Solution

	Alpha	Beta
Usage quantity	35,250	26,225
Unit cost	£2	£3
Purchase cost	£70,500	£78,675
(Usage quantity × unit cost)		

EXAMPLE – direct labour (utilisation and cost) budget

The direct labour utilisation budget will be based upon the production budget, taking into account the budgeted direct labour hours per unit of output to ascertain the direct labour utilisation. Once labour utilisation is determined the budgeted rate per hour may be applied to establish total direct labour cost.

Using the production budget example data, determine the labour budget assuming that two categories of labour are used: assemblers and finishers. The standard times per unit and budgeted standard unit rates are as follows:

	Assemblers (£6.00/hr)	Finishers (£7.00/hr)
Product A	5 hrs	2 hrs
Product D	2 hrs	3 hrs
Product G	1 hr	3 hrs

Solution

	Production (units)	Assemblers (total hrs)	Finishers (total hrs)
Product A	3,100	15,500	6,200
Product D	4,050	8,100	12,150
Product G	5,075	5,075	15,225
Total utilisation	–	28,675	33,575
Std rate/hr	–	£6.00/hr	£7.00/hr
Total labour cost	–	£172,050	£235,025

Other functional budgets

Other functional budgets such as selling and distribution, administration and so on may be derived once the budgets outlined above have been produced. Budgets for research and development and capital expenditure have some association with the budgets already discussed, but may not be integrated to the same degree.

Cash budgets

Cash budgets are of the utmost importance to an organisation. They provide details of all expected cash receipts and anticipated cash payments, usually month by month for the budget period. Cash flow and liquidity are paramount to the survival and the long-term viability of an organisation, as it must have sufficient cash to settle debts as they fall due. Where a cash budget identifies a shortfall in cash, arrangements may be made with bankers for an overdraft, or loan. Where the cash deficiency is likely to be long term, other forms of long-term finance may be arranged. Where a cash surplus is identified, investment opportunities may be undertaken. Cash budgets typically adopt a columnar approach and are an ideal spreadsheet application. A cash budget is an example of a *rolling budget*. As actual cost information becomes available it is possible to re-project the cash budget for the budget period.

Profit and cash surpluses are not the same. For example,

- Cash may be obtained from a loan or share issue, this is unrelated to profit.
- Cash may be paid for the purchase of fixed assets. The charge in the financial accounts would be for the proportion of the asset known as depreciation.
- Purchases and sales are usually made on credit. The cash transaction may take place some time after goods have been received or supplied.

An example cash budget layout is as follows:

	Jan	Feb	Mar	Apr	May	Jun	Jul	Aug	Sep	Oct	Nov	Dec
Receipts												
Debtors-sales												
Loans received												
Share issue												
Sale of assets												
Total receipts												
Payments												
Wages												
Salaries												
Creditors-purchases												
Purchase of assets												
Loan payments												
Total payments												
Opening cash balance												
Net receipts/(payments)												
Closing cash balance												

Once the opening cash balance is recorded, the net cash receipts or payments is added or deducted respectively to arrive at a closing cash balance, which is the opening cash balance for the following period.

EXAMPLE

A company has a cash balance of £15,000 on 1 January. It is anticipated that a tax demand of £25,000 will be settled in March and that new equipment will be purchased for £15,000 in April and June. Sales are estimated at £30,000 per month, customers taking one month's credit. Purchases are estimated at £16,500 per month, which includes a discount for immediate payment. Salaries are estimated at £9000 for the first six months rising to £9500 from July. In February a loan of £45,000 must be repaid. A new loan of £65,000 will be received in September.

Prepare a cash budget for the year, analysed by months. Highlight the maximum overdraft that will be required by the company and determine the estimated year-end cash balance.

Solution

Receipts	Jan	Feb	Mar	Apr	May	Jun	Jul	Aug	Sep	Oct	Nov	Dec
Debtors-sales		30000	30000	30000	30000	30000	30000	30000	30000	30000	30000	30000
Loans received									65000			
Total receipts	0	30000	30000	30000	30000	30000	30000	30000	95000	30000	30000	30000
Payments												
Tax			25000									
Salaries	9000	9000	9000	9000	9000	9000	9500	9500	9500	9500	9500	9500
Creditors-purchases	16500	16500	16500	16500	16500	16500	16500	16500	16500	16500	16500	16500
Purchase of assets				15000		15000						
Loan payments		45000										
Total payments	25500	70500	50500	40500	25500	40500	26000	26000	26000	26000	26000	26000
Opening cash balance	15000	−10500	−51000	−71500	−82000	−77500	−88000	−84000	−80000	−11000	−7000	−3000
Net receipt/payment	−25500	−40500	−20500	−10500	4500	−10500	4000	4000	69000	4000	4000	4000
Closing cash balance	−10500	−51000	−71500	−82000	−77500	**−88000**	−84000	−80000	−11000	−7000	−3000	1000

The maximum overdraft requirement of £88,000 will occur in June. The estimated year-end cash balance is £1000.

FURTHER EXAMPLE

Using the data above, now assume that payments to creditors may be delayed by one month and that a further short-term loan of £30,000 may be obtained for 3 months commencing July.

Prepare a revised cash budget for the year, analysed by months. Highlight the maximum overdraft that will be required by the company and determine the revised estimated year-end cash balance.

Solution

Receipts	Jan	Feb	Mar	Apr	May	Jun	Jul	Aug	Sep	Oct	Nov	Dec
Debtors-sales		30000	30000	30000	30000	30000	30000	30000	30000	30000	30000	30000
Loans received							30000		65000			
Total receipts	0	30000	30000	30000	30000	30000	60000	30000	95000	30000	30000	30000
Payments												
Tax			25000									
Salaries	9000	9000	9000	9000	9000	9000	9500	9500	9500	9500	9500	9500
Creditors-purchases		16500	16500	16500	16500	16500	16500	16500	16500	16500	16500	16500
Purchase of assets				15000		15000						
Loan payments		45000								30000		
Total payments	9000	70500	50500	40500	25500	40500	26000	26000	26000	56000	26000	26000
Opening cash balance	15000	6000	−34500	−55000	−65500	−61000	−71500	−37500	−33500	35500	9500	13500
Net receipt/payment	−9000	−40500	−20500	−10500	4500	−10500	34000	4000	69000	−26000	4000	4000
Closing cash balance	6000	−34500	−55000	−65500	−61000	**−71500**	−37500	−33500	35500	9500	13500	17500

The maximum overdraft requirement of £71,500 will still occur in June. The estimated year-end cash balance is now £17,500.

Budgeting and uncertainty

Budgeting is part of the planning process for any organisation and relates to the future. The future is, however, uncertain and may not be able to be predicted with accuracy. It must be borne in mind that certain costs within a business may be more volatile and more prone to fluctuation; this must be acknowledged in the process. As a consequence it may be necessary to amend or revise a budget later when more certain information becomes available. There are various techniques available to deal with uncertainty in budgeting, including probabilities, simulation, sensitivity analysis and so on. A discussion of these techniques is beyond the scope of this text, but it is worth mentioning that such techniques do not remove the uncertainty inherent in predicting the future.

Sources of data for budgeting

The sources and availability of information for budgeting will vary according to the budget being prepared. Information may be available internally or may have to be sourced externally. The sources of information for a particular budget are likely to vary for different organisations.

Examples of budgets and possible sources of data

Some examples of the commonly produced budgets together with possible sources of information are given below.

- **Sales budget**   Source: marketing/sales function. This forecasting exercise takes into consideration price/demand relationships, economy factors, and sales/marketing costs.

   The sales forecast would take into account:

   – industry factors: competition prices, historical sales trend, total market;
   – firm's factors: sales effort, product price, credit policy, share of the market.

- **Production budget**   Source: Production management. Management would consider potential production volume given constraints that may exist, e.g. machine availability, labour capacity, stock holding policy. In determining the budgeted production level, management would consider the sales budget and stock holding requirements.

- **Raw material budget**   Once an estimate of production is completed, consideration of what raw materials are needed and what stock levels are required may take place. The raw material budget process would involve consideration of economic order quantities, maximum/minimum levels of stock, availability of working capital, discounts for bulk purchase.

- **Labour budget**   This would be based upon production estimates, and requires communication with the personnel department on recruitment/redundancy policy. The availability of skilled staff may also have an impact on whether staff may have to be outsourced/subcontracted.

- **Production overhead budget**   This will involve determining overheads for the specific output/activity levels. Therefore, total costs must be split between fixed and variable. Overheads may be analysed in detail, e.g. power, maintenance, indirect labour, to facilitate absorption rates (or equivalent) being determined.

   For example,

$$\text{Variable overhead absorption rate} = \frac{\text{Variable overhead (budgeted)}}{\text{Budgeted activity}}$$

$$\text{Fixed overhead absorption rate} = \frac{\text{Fixed overhead (budgeted)}}{\text{Budgeted activity}}$$

Rolling budgets

A rolling or continuous budget is particularly beneficial where conditions are volatile and where financial data is likely to change regularly. In such circumstances it may not be practicable to attempt to predict so far into the future as (say) 12 months.

A rolling budget would be prepared in detail for (say) the first three months with less detail for the remainder of the year. As each month is completed a further month's detail is added such that there is always a detailed budget available for the next three months. Such budgets are likely to be more accurate, realistic and attainable and promote more acceptance amongst staff as a result, but they will require considerably more work to constantly prepare.

Budgetary control

A budget is a plan of what the organisation has set itself to achieve translated into financial data. For any plan to be achieved it must be monitored and controlled to ensure that the organisation is on target to achieve it or to initiate appropriate control action to get back on course in the event of deviation. Once prepared and implemented, budgets must be monitored to ensure that they are adhered to, or where there is a significant deviation from budget that action is taken to prevent it from continuing. Appropriate managers must be assigned the responsibility for budget monitoring and ensuring that actual costs and revenues are monitored against budget in order that significant deviations from plan are identified as soon as possible so that corrective action may be taken.

Budgeting appraisal

Advantages
The advantages of budgeting are as follows:

- Budgets provide a mechanism for translating the organisation's strategic plan into attainable financial objectives.
- Budgets communicate financial objectives to staff in the organisation.
- The budgetary process provides an opportunity for staff to participate in the formulation of plans for the organisation. This may encourage goal congruence.
- Integrated budgets provide an opportunity to relate the activities in one function of the business to the activities in another function.
- Business objectives are more likely to be realised if they are quantified, measurable, achievable and communicated to staff in a timely manner.
- Budgetary control provides an opportunity for exception reporting with management focusing on significant or material deviations from plan.

Limitations
The limitations of budgeting are as follows:

- Budgets may become out of date quickly in volatile conditions.

- The budgetary process can prove to be time consuming and expensive.
- Staff may not accept (internalise) the budget established and may behave in a dysfunctional manner to ensure that objectives are not achieved.
- There may be a tendency to adhere to the budget rather than to take advantage of new opportunities that emerge.
- There may be a tendency to base the budget on last year's budget, with only minimal adjustments for price inflation and similar factors, rather than to prepare a realistic and feasible financial plan of what the business seeks to achieve.

Zero based budgeting

Zero based budgeting (ZBB) was developed to overcome some of the criticisms levelled at 'traditional' budgeting, where the tendency may be only to increment last year's budget for inflation and similar factors. ZBB takes a cost/benefit analysis approach to budgeting. Each item of expenditure commences at zero and a manager must justify the expenditure based upon the benefits it is likely to derive. For example, the expenditure for an entire department or function may commence at zero and the activities of that part of the business be clearly evaluated to determine the benefits before expenditure may increase from zero to the desired level. This fundamental reappraisal of all business activities along cost/benefit lines forces managers to reappraise the contribution a department or function is making to the business. Given that resources are finite for all businesses, ZBB allows them to be prioritised according to the greatest benefits derived. ZBB has proved popular with not-for-profit organisations and government bodies, where the output may be more difficult to quantify. Manufacturing companies have tended to confine ZBB to service and support activities.

Steps in implementing ZBB

The following steps are involved:

1 Managers specify 'decision units', a unit may be an area of activity, capital expenditure etc. A decision unit must be able to be individually evaluated.
2 Decision units are elaborated on in a 'decision package'. Decision packages describe an activity in such a way that management may evaluate and rank it using cost/benefit analysis.
3 Decision packages are ranked using cost/benefit analysis.
4 Activities where the cost is greater than the benefit are excluded.

5 The resources available to the organisation are allocated according to the ranking.

Advantages

It is claimed that ZBB has the following advantages:

- it identifies and removes operations which are inefficient;
- it encourages the avoidance of wasteful expenditure;
- detailed knowledge of the organisation is required;
- once a decision package is approved, managers become committed to the success of the budget;
- it results in a fundamental reappraisal of all business activities;
- it results in a more efficient and equitable allocation of scarce resources.

Disadvantages

The following are claimed to be disadvantages of ZBB:

- the emphasis is on short-term returns as opposed to long-term benefits;
- it pre-supposes that commitments for expenditure are made at budget time;
- cost/benefit analysis may prove problematic, particularly with qualitative rather than quantitative data;
- it is a time-consuming exercise.

Activity based budgeting

Activity based budgeting (ABB) is sometimes referred to as activity based cost management and is based upon the principles established for activity based costing (ABC). You will recall from Chapter 7 that a category of overhead, long-term variable costs, did not vary with the volume of production or service, but did vary with some other measure of activity. Overheads were related to the activities that cause or 'drive' them with the use of cost drivers. Budgeted cost drivers, budgeted volumes and budgeted overhead may be used to determine the budgeted overhead for a particular activity in a given period. Cost driver volumes and budgeted overhead may then be monitored and reported to management on an exception basis. Whilst it is acknowledged that controlling a particular cost driver is unlikely to reduce overhead in the short term, by focusing management's attention on significant non-value added activities which are increasing, it is hoped that over a period of time costs would be reduced or at least controlled.

Summary

- A budget is a plan of action expressed in financial terms relating to a future period:
    - It should encompass all of the activities of the business.
    - It should involve personnel throughout the organisation.
- The preparation of a budget will facilitate:
    - planning,
    - coordination,
    - motivation,
    - communication,
    - control.
- The budget must operate within the organisational framework.
    - It must overlay the organisational structure.
- Budgets are prepared for a particular period of time identified at the outset.
    - This is referred to as the budget period.
- Budgets would be prepared from strategic plans.
    - Top management would develop a master budget.
    - Other staff would develop detailed functional budgets.
- No part of the business should prepare its budgets in isolation.
    - Budgets are integrated.
    - Integration encourages coordination of individual department's activities.
- There are several steps in constructing an integrated budget.
    - All major functional budgets must be included.
    - There may be an order of preparation for functional budgets.
- Cash budgets are of paramount importance to an organisation.
    - Cash flow and liquidity must be planned and monitored if an organisation is to have sufficient cash to meet its financial obligations as they fall due.
- Once budgets are agreed and implemented, they must be adhered to.
    - Budgets must be monitored and controlled.
    - Significant exceptions should be reported to management for further investigation.
- An alternative to traditional 'incremental' budgeting is zero based budgeting.
    - ZBB takes a cost/benefit analysis approach to budgeting.
    - Only those parts of the organisation that can demonstrate viability using cost/benefit analysis techniques would receive an allocation of resources.

- ZBB is particularly popular with not-for-profit organisations and government bodies.

● Activity based budgeting uses the principles of ABC for budgeting.
  - The use of budgeted cost driver volumes and budgeted overhead may help to determine the overhead for a particular activity.

Questions for review

1 What is a budget?

2 Explain the significance of a strategic plan to the preparers of budgets.

3 What is an integrated budget? Illustrate your answer with an example.

4 Using an appropriate diagram, discuss the budgetary process.

5 Discuss the significance of the organisational framework for budgeting.

6 Explain the role of a budget committee in budget preparation.

7 Explain the significance of a cash budget for an organisation.

8 Give *three* examples where profit and cash are not the same.

9 Define a rolling budget.

10 From a behavioural point of view, what is an optimum budget?

11 Discuss how budgets may be achieved, once implemented.

12 Give *three* advantages of budgeting.

13 Give *three* disadvantages of budgeting.

14 Describe how ZBB may overcome some of the limitations of traditional incremental budgeting.

15 Define ABB.

Self-assessment questions

(*Denotes that a suggested solution may be found at the end of this book.)

1* Rolling budgets discussion
Discuss how rolling budgets may be beneficial for planning and control.

2* Budgeted cost data
A company has just commenced production of a new product. At the end of the period, it wishes to have 250 units in stock. Budgeted sales are 4500 units.

Due to a problem in the production process 5% of the completed production will not comply with the specification and will need to be scrapped. Scrapped units may be sold for £5/unit.

Cost data is as follows:

	£/unit
Labour	18
Material	10

a Determine the budgeted material and labour cost for the period.

b Calculate the scrap value of units.

3 Motivational aspects of budgeting

Discuss the importance of motivation and goal congruence for budgeting and budgetary control.

Chapter 11

Standard costing and variance analysis

Chapter objectives

Having studied this chapter, you should be able to:

- explain the term standard cost;
- understand the relationship between standard costs and budgets;
- subdivide a cost variance into constituent components;
- appreciate the difference between adverse and favourable variances;
- compute labour, material and overhead variances;
- suggest reasons for the cause of variances;
- appreciate the limitations of standard costing and variance analysis;
- be aware of the behavioural aspects of standard costing and variance analysis.

Introduction

The purpose of this chapter is to introduce standard costing and variance analysis, which is widely used in practice and an appreciation of which is paramount for the cost accountant. It is a very sophisticated technique, which may be applied to a variety of organisations. Rather than covering the technique comprehensively here, addressing all possible variance calculations, we will introduce direct cost and overhead variances only, concentrating on the principles of calculation, interpreting the variances and the reconciliation of budgeted to actual cost.

Standard costing is related to budgeting in that a standard cost is a predetermined cost prepared in advance. Standard costs may be calculated for labour, material and fixed and variable overhead. Once predetermined costs are established, they may be compared with the actual costs for the period and the difference or variance may be recorded. If the variance is significant it would be reported to management as it may warrant further investigation. Variances may be subdivided into sub-components as part of any analysis; this is referred to as variance analysis.

Variance analysis is an important mechanism in a 'control feedback reporting system'. When it is *material* or significant, information on 'off standard performance' is fed back to management for further investigation. Standard costing and variance analysis follows the principles of exception reporting.

Standard costing is widely used in manufacturing and service industries and is particularly appropriate for organisations that carry out repetitive tasks (e.g. cleaning, refuse collection, public transport).

The basis of standard costing is flexible budgeting, i.e. budgeting on a unit basis rather than a total basis, and allowing the budget to be flexed to the actual level of activity or output, prior to comparing the flexed budget with the actual cost. A standard cost is therefore a realistic and attainable target and not an average of past costs. Standards should be regularly reviewed to reflect changes in prices, technology and methods employed, if the subsequent variances are to be of any value for control purposes.

In this chapter we will address the setting of standard costs and the motivational aspects. The calculation of the most common variances will be illustrated and the value of such calculations will be discussed, together with possible reasons for off standard performance.

What is a standard cost?

A standard cost is an attainable cost for an activity determined on a unit basis (e.g. labour cost per car manufactured, or per dustbin emptied). A standard cost is expressed in financial terms and is recorded for each activity that an organisation may carry out. Standards are carefully prepared to reflect current prices and prevailing operating conditions. For standard costing to be successful, the costs determined must be accepted (internalised) by the managers responsible for controlling those costs. The setting of standards will involve extensive discussion between the cost accountant and the appropriate manager concerned in order that the standard arrived at is accepted by all as being achievable. If standards are not realistic and feasible, personnel are unlikely to strive to achieve them. This would result in a meaningless performance measure. Standards may be periodically revised. This tends to be an annual exercise for many organisations, but clearly if the company operates in a volatile market, where costs are likely to fluctuate significantly over a shorter period of time, it may be necessary to revise the standards more frequently.

What is variance analysis?

A variance is the difference between the standard cost for an item of production or the provision of a service, and the actual cost of the same.

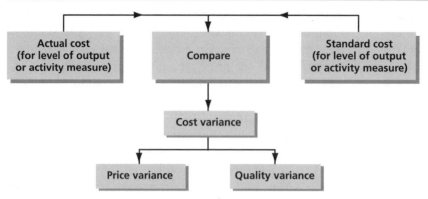

Figure 19 Cost variances

Cost variances are normally produced for labour, materials and overhead; each cost variance may be subdivided into a price and quantity component. Figure 19 illustrates this.

Variances may be:

- **adverse (adv)** the actual cost is greater than the standard cost;
- **favourable (fav)** the actual cost is less than the standard cost.

Variance reports should highlight significant variances, both adverse and favourable to assist management to control the operations of the enterprise. Management may use such information to:

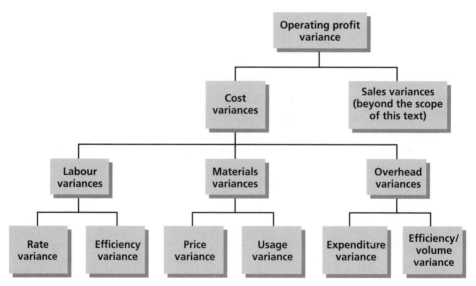

Figure 20 Hierarchy of variances

- stop the deviation from plan for adverse variances;
- exploit deviations from plan for favourable variances.

Variances form a hierarchy to the operating profit variance. See Figure 20.

Total cost variances are subdivided into a price and quantity variance using the following terminology:

- **Cost element**
  - material
  - labour
  - overhead
- **Price variance**
  - price
  - rate
  - expenditure
- **Quantity variance**
  - usage
  - efficiency
  - efficiency/volume

Variance calculation

It is now appropriate to demonstrate the calculation of variances and to offer some explanations as to their possible causes. An example of variance calculation for each cost element is shown below.

Material and labour variances

The material cost variance will involve comparing the actual cost of material with the standard material cost for the actual level of production or activity. Similarly, the labour cost variance will involve comparing the actual cost of labour with the standard labour cost for the actual level of production or activity.

EXAMPLE

A company manufactures product 2. The standard cost for this product is as follows:

Direct material used	3 kg/unit
Direct material cost	£1.50 per kg
Direct labour cost	£5 per hour
Direct labour time	30 minutes per unit

The actual data for the product is as follows:

Actual production	10 units
Actual materials used	40 kg
Actual material cost	£56
Actual labour time	6 hours
Actual labour cost	£35

1 Determine the standard cost of product 2.

2 Determine the actual cost for product 2.

3 Determine the flexed budget for product 2.

4 Determine the total variance for product 2.

5 Calculate the following:

   a Material price variance
   b Material usage variance
   c Material total variance
   d Labour rate variance
   e Labour efficiency variance
   f Labour total variance.

Solution

1 Standard cost of product 2

		£
Material	3 kg/unit × £1.50/kg	4.50
Labour	30 minutes/unit × £5/hr	2.50
Standard cost/unit		7.00

2 Actual cost for product 2

		£
Material	40 kg cost	56
Labour	6 hours cost	35
Actual costs		91

3 Flexed budget for product 2
Standard cost/unit × Actual production (£7 × 10 units) = £70

4 Total variance for product 2
Flexed budget – actual cost of product 2 (£70 – £91) = (£21)*
  * Brackets indicate an adverse variance

5 a Material price variance

Actual material cost (from question)	£56	
Actual materials @ standard price (40 kg × £1.50)	£60	£4 fav

b Material usage variance

Actual materials @ standard price (40 kg × £1.50)	£60	
Standard materials* @ standard price (3 kg × £1.50 × 10 units)	£45	(£15) adv

  * for the actual level of activity

c Materials total variance (Price variance + usage variance)   (£11) adv

d Labour rate variance

Actual labour cost (from question)	£35	
Actual labour hrs @ standard rate: (6 hrs × £5)	£30	(£5) adv

e Labour efficiency variance

Actual labour hrs @ standard rate (6 hrs × £5)   £30

Standard labour hrs* @ standard rate (0.5 hr × £5 × 10 units)   £25   (£5) adv

* for the actual level of activity

f Labour total variance (rate variance + efficiency variance)   (£10) adv

The net total of the individual cost variances above should reconcile to the total variance calculated in question 4 earlier.

	£	
Material total variance	(11)	adv
Labour total variance	(10)	adv
Total variance	(21)	adv

This is the same as calculated in question 4 (total variance = flexed budget − actual cost).

The total variance of £21 (adverse) indicated the extent to which a budgeted profit would not be achieved in practice. This total variance was subdivided between a materials total variance of £11 (adverse) and a labour total variance of £10 (adverse). Each of these total variances was further subdivided into a price and usage component in the case of materials, and rate and efficiency in the case of labour. This subdivision would enable management to determine whether the increase in cost compared with standard was as a result of a quantity increase (too much material used or too many labour hours worked) or as a consequence of materials costing more than planned or labour being paid a higher rate than planned. Such information is vital to management in controlling the costs of an organisation.

Overhead variances (marginal and absorption)

Before discussing overhead variances, it is worth reiterating the difference in treatment of overhead under marginal and absorption costing. You will recall from Chapter 6 that absorption costing treats overhead as a product cost or a service cost, including a proportion of overhead into each unit manufactured or each unit of service delivered. Whereas marginal costing treats overhead as a period cost, or fixed cost. In the latter case the overhead is included in the period in which it was incurred and no attempt is made to include a proportion of this cost into units of production or service. This fundamental difference in the treatment of overhead has both stock valuation and profit implications and this was demonstrated in Chapter 6, but it also has implications for standard costing and variance analysis, with slightly a different approach being adopted depending on whether marginal or absorption costing is used.

The treatment of overhead (fixed costs) using a marginal costing approach requires that only a fixed overhead expenditure variance be calculated. Variable overhead variances are calculated in the same manner irrespective of whether marginal or absorption costing is used, as these costs do vary with some activity or output measure. An explanation of overhead variances under absorption costing is given below. Further discussion of standard marginal costing is beyond the scope of this book, the main focus being standard absorption costing where a full range of fixed overhead variances may be calculated, including the expenditure variance referred to above.

Overhead variances absorption costing

Where overhead variances are calculated, it is usual to adopt an absorption costing approach. You will recall that under absorption costing, overhead absorption rates were determined in advance. It is these absorption rates that provide the standard cost for overhead. For the purpose of variance analysis, a separate absorption rate is determined for fixed and variable overheads as follows:

$$\text{Fixed overhead absorption rate (FOAR)} = \frac{\text{Budgeted fixed overhead}}{\text{Budgeted activity measure}}$$

$$\text{Variable overhead absorption rate (VOAR)} = \frac{\text{Budgeted variable overhead}}{\text{Budgeted activity measure}}$$

The variable overhead total variance will involve a comparison between the actual variable overheads for the period and the variable overhead absorbed. This total variance may be subdivided into an expenditure variance and an efficiency variance.

- **Expenditure variance** A comparison between the actual variable overhead and the variable overhead absorbed based upon the actual hours worked.

- **Efficiency variance** A comparison between the variable overhead based upon the actual hours worked and the absorbed variable overhead.

The fixed overhead total variance will involve a comparison between the fixed costs for the period and the standard fixed costs for the output or activity level achieved. This variance may be subdivided into an expenditure variance and a volume variance.

- **Expenditure variance** A comparison between the actual fixed overhead and the budgeted fixed overhead for the period.

- **Volume variance** A comparison between the standard cost of overhead absorbed for the level of output or activity achieved and the budget for the period.

Overhead variances do not provide the same type of useful control information provided by direct cost variances, this is because they are reliant upon the overhead absorption process in the determination of FOAR and VOAR. Variances arise as a consequence of a change in the budgeted levels of overhead or activity measure used to determine the absorption rate. In practice overhead variances are not calculated as frequently as direct cost variances as the value of such variances to management for control purposes is debatable.

EXAMPLE

A company manufactures product y. The budgeted overhead costs for period 6 were as follows:

Fixed overhead	£15,180
Variable overhead	£13,500
Labour hours	3000 hrs

The actual overhead costs for period 6 were as follows:

Fixed overhead	£15,250
Variable overhead	£13,100
Labour hours worked	3300 hrs
Standard labour hours produced*	3500 hrs
* for the actual level of activity	

1 Determine the FOAR and VOAR.

2 Determine the variable overhead variances.

3 Determine the fixed overhead variances.

Solution

1 $FOAR = \dfrac{£15,180}{3000 \text{ hrs}} = £5.06/\text{hr}$

$VOAR = \dfrac{£13,500}{3000 \text{ hrs}} = £4.50/\text{hr}$

2

			£	£
a	Variable overhead expenditure variance			
	Actual variable overhead		13,100	
	Actual labour hours @ VOAR	(3300 hrs × £4.50)	14,850	1,750 fav
b	Variable overhead efficiency variance			
	Actual labour hours @ VOAR	(3300 hrs × £4.50)	14,850	
	Standard labour hours* @ VOAR	(3500 hrs × £4.50)	15,750	900 fav
	* for the actual level of activity			
c	Variable overhead total variance			2,650 fav

3

   a Fixed overhead expenditure variance   £   £

		£	£
a Fixed overhead expenditure variance			
Actual fixed overhead		15,250	
Budgeted fixed overhead		15,180	(70) adv
b Fixed overhead volume variance			
Budgeted fixed overhead		15,180	
Standard labour hours* @ FOAR	(3500 hrs × £5.06)	17,710	2,530 fav
* for the actual level of activity			
c Fixed overhead total variance			2,460 fav

Reasons for variances

Some of the most common reasons for direct cost variances arising are as follows:

- **Labour rates**

  - Wage rate changed.
  - Alternative level of skilled labour used.
  - The standard may be in error.

- **Materials price**

  - Inflation.
  - Alternative supplier used.
  - Different grade of material used.
  - Changes in shipping/delivery costs.
  - The standard may be in error.

- **Labour efficiency**

  - Quality of material.
  - Alternative level of skilled labour used.
  - Machinery malfunction.
  - Inappropriate supervision.
  - The standard may be in error.

- **Material usage**

  - Poor product specification.
  - Quality of material.
  - Material deterioration in stock.
  - The standard may be in error.

Variance investigation

Variance analysis provides useful feedback control information for off standard performance. Some of the possible reasons for direct cost variances were outlined in the section above. However, to determine the reasons why a particular variance, or a group of variances, have occurred, may require a technical investigation of a production process or service operation; this may be time-consuming and expensive.

Before a variance investigation is undertaken the following points are worth considering:

- a focus on material/significant variances;
- whether the variances indicate a correctable problem;
- the costs incurred in making an investigation;
- the costs incurred in not correcting a correctable problem;
- the trend of variances.

The variances themselves may provide some insight into what the particular reasons are. It may be possible to identify interrelationships between variances, which may provide additional information as to their likely cause. For example, an adverse labour efficiency variance and a favourable material price variance may indicate the purchase of a cheaper and hence poorer quality material that has resulted in longer production time as a consequence.

Appraisal of standard costing and variance analysis

Advantages

- It is management by exception: by studying variances, management's attention is directed to those areas of the business which are not proceeding according to plan.
- Management is able to delegate cost control, via the standard costing system.
- The process of setting, revising and monitoring standards encourages re-appraisal of methods, materials and techniques.
- With full participation from management it encourages goal congruence.

Disadvantages

- It is expensive and time-consuming to install and keep up to date.
- In volatile conditions, rates and prices soon become out of date.
- Many variances are not understood by managers.

- The usefulness of some variances (e.g. overhead variances) is questionable.
- Variance analysis and subsequent investigation are post mortems of past events.

Summary

- A standard cost is expressed in financial terms and is an attainable cost for an activity.
  - Standard costs are determined on a unit basis.
- A variance is the difference between the standard cost of an item of production, or provision of the service, and the actual cost of the same. Variances may be:
  - adverse (actual cost greater than standard cost);
  - favourable (actual cost less than standard cost).
- The following cost variances are normally produced:
  - material: price and usage;
  - labour: rate and efficiency;
  - variable overhead: expenditure and efficiency;
  - fixed overhead: expenditure and volume.
- Variance reports should highlight significant variances, both adverse and favourable, to assist management to:
  - stop deviation from plan for adverse variances;
  - exploit deviation from plan for favourable variances.
- Variances form a hierarchy to the operating profit variance.
  - Budgeted and actual performance may be reconciled using variance analysis.
- The setting of appropriate standards will involve extensive dialogue between the cost accountant and the appropriate manager.
  - The standard arrived at must be realistic and feasible and accepted by all.
  - Standards may be periodically revised.
- To determine why a particular variance has occurred a technical investigation of the production process or the service may be necessary. Management should take into account:
  - material/significant variances,
  - whether the variances indicate a correctable problem,
  - the costs incurred in making an investigation,
  - the costs incurred in not correcting a correctable problem,
  - the trend of variances.

Questions for review

1 What is a standard cost?

2 Explain the process of variance analysis.

3 What is an adverse variance? Illustrate your answer with an example.

4 What is a favourable variance? Illustrate your answer with an example.

5 Using an appropriate diagram, describe how variances form a hierarchy to the operating profit variance.

6 Discuss the significance of the flexed budget for standard costing and variance analysis.

7 Give *three* examples of reasons for direct labour rate variances.

8 Give *three* examples of reasons for direct labour efficiency variances.

9 Give *three* examples of reasons for direct material price variances.

10 Give *three* examples of reasons for direct material usage variances.

11 From a behavioural point of view, what is an optimum standard cost?

12 Discuss what matters may be taken into consideration prior to a technical investigation of variances being undertaken.

13 Discuss how the interrelationships of variances may be significant in any variance investigation.

14 Give *three* advantages of standard costing.

15 Give *three* disadvantages of standard costing.

Self-assessment questions

(*Denotes that a suggested solution may be found at the end of this book.)

1 **Standard costing and planning and control**
   Discuss how standard costing and variance analysis may be beneficial for planning and control.

2* **Material variances**
   A company has just commenced production of a new product.
   The standard costs for material are as follows:

   Standard consumption per unit   3 kg
   Standard price per kg of material   £1.40

The actual production for period 1 was 10 units. The actual material costs were:

Actual consumption per unit	4 kg
Actual price per kg of material	£1.50

Determine the material price and usage variances for period 1.

3* Variance determination and calculation
Determine all relevant variances from the following data.
  The standard costs for material are as follows:

Standard consumption per unit	5 cm
Standard price per cm of material	£0.50

The actual production for period 5 was 100 units. The actual material costs were £250 for 420 cm.

4* Interpreting variances
XY plc produces a vegetarian product in tins that is retailed nationally. It was established that the standard costs were as follows for the period in question:

Materials	12 soya pieces per unit at 56 pence per piece
Labour	2 hours per unit at £2.75 per hour

During the month of November, the company produced 1000 tins of the product. The information that relates to this production was as follows:

Materials	15,000 soya pieces at total cost of £7250
Labour	£8000
Direct labour hours worked	2500

There were no stocks at the beginning and end of November.
  Compute the material price and usage variances and labour rate and efficiency variances and write a brief report to the Board of Directors explaining the significance of each of the variances.

5 Flexed budget
The standard cost for one Acme axle based upon production of 1000 units per month is as follows:

	£
Direct labour	18
Direct material	15
Fixed overhead	17
	$\overline{50}$

The actual cost per unit for December when 1200 axles were made was as follows:

	£
Direct labour	17
Direct material	18
Fixed overhead	17
	52

Using a columnar approach, determine the total actual costs, flexed budget and all relevant variances for the Acme axle.

6* Variance calculation

A cabinet manufacturer has established standard costs for the joinery department producing bathroom cabinets:

		£
Material	timber 25 metres @ £0.20 per metre	5.00
Labour	1.2 hours of semi-skilled labour @ £4.75 per hour	5.70
Variable overhead	1.2 hours @ £1.50 per hour	1.80
Fixed overhead	1.2 hours @ £1.25 per hour	1.50
		14.00

In period 3, 1100 cabinets were produced. This was 100 more than anticipated. The actual costs for period 3 were as follows:

		£
Material	timber 25,000 metres @ £0.21 per metre	5,250
Labour	1200 hours labour @ £4.95 per hour	5,940
Variable overhead		950
Fixed overhead		1,350
		13,490

Compute all variances.

7 Motivational aspects of standard costing

Discuss the importance of motivation and internalisation of standards for standard costing and variance analysis.

Chapter 12

Capital investment appraisal

Chapter objectives

Having studied this chapter you should be able to:

- understand the importance of capital investment appraisal;
- understand the differences between short-term and long-term decision making;
- calculate the ARR of an investment;
- determine payback for a project;
- understand the concept of the time value of money;
- calculate the NPV and IRR for a project;
- appreciate the risk and uncertainty that is inherent in capital projects;
- appreciate the limitations of capital investment appraisal techniques.

Introduction

Capital investment appraisal is the study of long-term decision making. Capital expenditure is different from revenue expenditure (labour and material costs etc.). Capital expenditure is concerned with the purchase of large capital items such as new plant and equipment, a new office block, or perhaps the purchase of another company. The benefits derived from such purchases are likely to have an impact for several years.

The purpose of this chapter is to introduce long-term decision making. This is similar to short-term decision making in that it involves a choice between alternatives and the comparison of costs and revenues. However, because of the extended time horizon, uncertainty and inflation may also need to be borne in mind in the decision-making process.

Long-term decision making usually involves some form of capital investment appraisal, where there will be an initial investment into a project possibly followed by subsequent investments. The returns from the project are likely to be over several periods (typically years) and given the extended time period, the level of uncertainty and risk is likely to be greater than for short-term decisions.

This chapter will examine the most commonly used capital investment appraisal techniques and discuss their usefulness as an aid to decision making.

What is capital investment appraisal?

Capital investment appraisal is a technique whereby long-term capital projects may be considered to determine whether such projects are financially viable and worth undertaking, or to determine the relative financial viability where there is a choice between alternative competing projects.

The principal capital investment appraisal methods are:

- accounting rate of return (ARR)
- payback method
- net present value (NPV)
- internal rate of return (IRR).

Both ARR and the payback method are conventional capital investment appraisal techniques, whereas the NPV and IRR are discounted cash flow (DCF) techniques and involve the important concept of the *time value of money*.

Conventional capital investment appraisal techniques

Accounting rate of return (ARR)

The accounting rate of return attempts to measure the returns of a project with the capital investment for the same. An assessment of project viability requires the following formula:

$$\text{ARR} = \frac{\text{Estimated average profit}}{\text{Estimated average investment}} \times 100\%$$

EXAMPLE

A company is considering the purchase of a new machine. There are two types available in the market, X and Y. Data relating to the initial cost and returns from the machines are given below.

	Machine X (£)	Machine Y (£)
Cost	(12,000)	(10,000)
Asset life	4 yrs	4 yrs
Residual value	2,000	3,000
Future profits		
Yr1	7,000	1,500
Yr2	4,000	2,000
Yr3	2,000	2,000
Yr4	1,000	1,000

Based upon the accounting rate of return, which machine should be purchased?

Solution

	Machine X (£)	Machine Y (£)
Total profits	14,000	6,500
Asset life	4 yrs	4 yrs
Average profits (÷4)	**3,500**	**1,625**
Value of investment at start	12,000	10,000
Value of investment at end	2,000	3,000
	14,000	13,000
Average investment (÷2)	**7,000**	**6,500**
ARR	$\frac{3,500}{7,000} = 50\%$	$\frac{1,625}{6,500} = 25\%$

Machine X should be chosen as it provides the highest accounting rate of return of 50% compared with machine Y with a return of 25%.

If only a single investment opportunity was being considered, the ARR could be compared with the opportunity cost of investing in the project. For example, could the investment provide a better return than other types of investments?

ARR appraisal

The following are claimed to be advantages of ARR:

- ease of calculation;
- it is easy to understand;

- data is often readily available;
- ease of comparison between projects as ARR uses a relative measure (percentage).

The following are claimed to be disadvantages of ARR:

- it is not based upon cash flows. It uses accounting profits which may contain subjective judgements for profit determination;
- it does not consider the timing of cash flows;
- there are a variety of ways in which capital employed may be calculated in practice.

Payback method

The payback method attempts to measure how quickly the cash inflows (as opposed to accounting profits) from an investment will pay back the initial cost of the investment. The project with the shortest payback period will be preferred. Consideration is therefore given to the timing of cash flows.

EXAMPLE

A company is considering the purchase of a new machine. There are two types available in the market, A and B. Data relating to the initial cost and returns from the machines are given below.

	Machine A (£)	Machine B (£)
Cost	(12,000)	(10,000)
Future cash inflows		
Yr1	7,000	6,500·
Yr2	2,000	3,500
Yr3	3,000	2,000
Yr4	8,000	1,000
Yr5	6,000	1,000

Based upon the payback method, which machine should be purchased?

Solution

	Machine A (£)	Machine B (£)
Cost	(12,000)	(10,000)
Future cash inflows		
Yr1	7,000	6,500
Yr2	2,000	> 3,500< payback
Yr3	> 3,000< payback	2,000
Yr4	8,000	1,000
Yr5	6,000	1,000
Total	26,000	14,000

Machine B should be chosen because the payback is at the end of year 2, whereas machine A pays back at the end of year 3. *However the returns from machine A are £12,000 greater than machine B.*

Payback appraisal

The following are claimed to be advantages of payback:

- ease of calculation;
- it is easy to understand;
- payback uses cash flows, rather than accounting profits;
- by choosing the project with the quickest payback, risk may be minimised;
- where returns are made sooner, these may be reinvested in other projects.

The following are claimed to be disadvantages of payback:

- it provides an indication of liquidity, but not project returns over the entire life of the project;
- it provides only a crude measure of the timings of cash flows;
- it does not consider the time value of money.

Discounted cash flow appraisal techniques

Discounted cash flow (DCF) considers cash flows rather than accounting profits and also takes into account the important aspect of the *time value of money*. Time value of money refers to the fact that cash received at different times must be adjusted to a present value using the prevailing cost of capital to reflect the time period that has passed.

In order to understand the necessity of considering the time value of money, we first need to consider compound interest calculations.

DCF and compound interest

A company invests £1000 at an interest rate of 10%.

- At the end of year 1 the investment is worth

  £1000 @ 10% = £1100

- At the end of year 2 the investment is worth

  £1100 @ 10% = £1210

The interest in year 2 is £1210 − £1100 = £110.

- At the end of year 3 the investment is worth

  £1210 @ 10% = £1331

The interest in year 3 is £1331 − £1210 = £121.

Discounted cash flow uses the principle of compound interest to determine a *present value* for future income. In the example above £1000 invested for three years at 10% compound interest is worth £1331 at the end of year 3.

An investor should therefore be indifferent as to whether to receive £1331 in three year's time or receive £1000 now (where the returns are known with certainty).

In other words £1331 received at the end of year 3 has a value today (present value) of £1000, at a 10% cost of capital.

The principle of DCF allows for forecast future income to be adjusted to today's value a present value whereupon it may be compared with the initial investment to determine whether it is financially viable.

There are two principal DCF techniques for capital investment appraisal:

- Net present value (NPV) This provides an absolute measure for project performance.
- Internal rate of return (IRR) This provides a relative measure for project performance.

Both of these techniques require that cash flows are adjusted or *discounted* to a present value and compared with the initial capital outlay. To discount future income streams by a given cost of capital the following discount factor formula is used:

$$\frac{1}{(1+r)^n}$$

where

r = rate of interest/cost of capital
n = number of years

For convenience, discount rates may be obtained from predetermined present value tables. Typically such tables would display cost of capital horizontally along the top of the table and the number of years vertically along the left-hand side of the table. Discount rates for a given cost of capital and number of years may be obtained from the main body of the table. For example, the discount rate for £1 for year 1 at 10% cost of capital is 0.909, year 2 is 0.826, year 3 is 0.751. As the discount rate is for £1 it must be multiplied by the cash flow in the particular year to determine the present value. A table of present value factors may be found in Appendix A.

Annuity tables are similar to present value tables and are used in a similar manner. The number of years in this case refers to the same amount (annuity) being received, or paid annually. A single present value annuity factor may be used in place of present value factors where the cash inflow/outflow is the same for a number of consecutive years. A table of annuity value factors may also be found in Appendix A.

Net present value (NPV)

The net present value (NPV) of an investment is the future income streams adjusted or discounted to a present value using the formula shown in the section above or the present value tables in Appendix A. The discount rate calculated from the formula or obtained from the table is for £1. It must therefore be multiplied by the cash flow in the particular year to determine the present value. Once a present value is determined for each year for the cash inflows it is compared with the initial capital outlay and an absolute value is determined. If the resultant NPV is positive, the project yields a greater return than the initial investment after adjusting for the time value of money and is therefore worth undertaking. The greater the NPV the more financially worthwhile the investment opportunity.

EXAMPLE

A company is considering the purchase of a new machine. There are two types available in the market, P and Q. Data relating to the initial cost and returns from the machines is given below. The company's cost of capital is 10%.

	Machine P (£)	Machine Q (£)
Cost (Yr0)	(12,000)	(10,000)
Future cash inflows		
Yr1	7,000	6,500
Yr2	2,000	3,500
Yr3	3,000	4,000
Yr4	8,000	1,000
Yr5	6,000	3,000

Based upon NPV, which machine should be purchased?

Solution

	Machine P (£)	10% discount factor	Present value (£)
Cost (Yr0)	(12,000)		(12,000)
Future cash inflows			
Yr1	7,000 ×	0.909 =	6,363
Yr2	2,000 ×	0.826 =	1,652
Yr3	3,000 ×	0.751 =	2,253
Yr4	8,000 ×	0.683 =	5,464
Yr5	6,000 ×	0.621 =	3,726
NPV			7,458

The forecast NPV of machine P is positive. Allowing for the cost of capital, the project yields a return greater than the initial investment and is therefore worth undertaking.

	Machine Q (£)	10% discount factor	Present value (£)
Cost (Yr0)	(10,000)		(10,000)
Future cash inflows			
Yr1	6,500 ×	0.909 =	5,908.50
Yr2	3,500 ×	0.826 =	2,891
Yr3	4,000 ×	0.751 =	3,004
Yr4	1,000 ×	0.683 =	683
Yr5	3,000 ×	0.621 =	1,863
NPV			4,349.50

The forecast NPV of machine Q is also positive. Allowing for the cost of capital, the project yields a return greater than the initial investment and is therefore worth undertaking.

Both investment opportunities provide a positive NPV and both are worth undertaking. Machine P should be chosen in preference to machine Q, as the forecast NPV is £7458 − £4349.5 = £3108.50 higher.

NPV appraisal

The following are claimed to be advantages of NPV:

- NPV uses cash flows, rather than accounting profits;
- it takes into account the time value of money;
- it considers the timings of cash flows;
- simple decision rule: if the NPV is positive the project is worth undertaking;
- where there is more than one alternative, projects may be ranked according to NPV.

The following are claimed to be disadvantages of NPV:

- predictions for cost of capital over the project life can prove problematic;
- it does not take into account the risk associated with later cash flows;
- it is more difficult to calculate and understand than 'traditional' investment appraisal techniques.

Internal rate of return (IRR)

Internal rate of return (IRR) uses DCF techniques in a similar manner to NPV. It differs from NPV in that it provides a relative measure (a percentage) as opposed to the absolute figure provided by NPV. As the cost of capital rises, the NPV of a project will fall. IRR determines the discount rate, which provides a zero NPV through a process called interpolation. This requires the calculation of NPV using substituted costs of capital to determine those costs of capital resulting in a small negative NPV and a small positive NPV. Where the NPV is neither positive nor negative, the cash inflows, taking into account the cost of capital, equal the investment. For a project to be viable, the IRR percentage determined must be greater than the cost of capital for the project.

EXAMPLE

A company is considering the purchase of a new machine, T. Data relating to the initial cost and returns from the machine is given below. The company's cost of capital is 10%.

	Machine T (£)
Cost (Yr0)	(12,000)
Future cash inflows	
Yr1	7,000
Yr2	2,000
Yr3	3,000
Yr4	2,000
Yr5	1,000

Based upon IRR, should the machine be purchased?

Solution

First, use different discount rates to determine a small positive NPV and a small negative NPV. (As the discount factor rises, the project return (NPV) will become smaller.)

	Machine T (£)		10% discount factor		Present value (£)
Cost (Yr0)	(12,000)				(12,000)
Future cash inflows					
Yr1	7,000	×	0.909	=	6,363
Yr2	2,000	×	0.826	=	1,652
Yr3	3,000	×	0.751	=	2,253
Yr4	2,000	×	0.683	=	1,366
Yr5	1,000	×	0.621	=	621
NPV					255

	Machine T (£)		12% discount factor		Present value (£)
Cost (Yr0)	(12,000)				(12,000)
Future cash inflows					
Yr1	7,000	×	0.893	=	6,251
Yr2	2,000	×	0.797	=	1,594
Yr3	3,000	×	0.712	=	2,136
Yr4	2,000	×	0.636	=	1,272
Yr5	1,000	×	0.567	=	567
NPV					(180)

Secondly, apply the data for the positive and negative NPV to the following interpolation formula to determine the IRR.

$$IRR = A + \left(\frac{a}{a+b} \times (B - A) \right)\%$$

where
A = discount rate which gives +ve NPV
B = discount rate which gives −ve NPV
a = the amount of +ve NPV
b = the amount of −ve NPV (ignore the minus sign)

$$IRR = 10\% + \left(\frac{255}{255 + 180} \times (12 - 10) \right)\%$$

$$= 10\% + (0.59 \times 2\%)$$

$$= 10\% + 1.18\%$$

$$IRR = 11.18\%$$

The forecast IRR of 11.18% is marginally above the cost of capital of 10%. Therefore the project is worth undertaking and the machine should be purchased.

NPV Appraisal

The following are claimed to be advantages of IRR:

- IRR uses cash flows, rather than accounting profits;
- it takes into account the time value of money;
- it considers the timings of cash flows;
- simple decision rule: if the IRR is above the cost of capital, the project is worth undertaking;
- where there is more than one alternative, projects may be ranked according to IRR.

The following are claimed to be disadvantages of IRR:

- predictions for cost of capital over the project life can prove problematic;
- it does not take into account the risk associated with later cash flows;
- it is more difficult to calculate and understand than 'traditional' investment appraisal techniques;
- it requires the use of an interpolation formulae.

Discounted cash flow: NPV vs. IRR

Both NPV and IRR use discounted cash flow techniques to appraise the time value of money. NPV provides an absolute measure of return, whereas IRR provides a relative measure of return and requires the use of an interpolation formula.

NPV and IRR will result in the same decisions as to whether to undertake a project. They may, however, give conflicting results where a number of projects are required to be ranked. In such circumstances NPV tends to be chosen in practice.

Risk and uncertainty

Capital investment appraisal relates to the future and the future can be uncertain. Capital appraisal techniques considered in this chapter do not make an assessment as to the risk or uncertainty associated with a particular investment, nor do they take into account shortcomings in forecasting future costs and revenues. It is important that management takes this into account in reaching any decision. There are techniques available to assist with this, such as sensitivity analysis, probabilities and standard deviation, but they are beyond the scope of this text.

Summary

- Capital investment appraisal is the study of long-term decision making.
  - Capital expenditure is concerned with the purchase of large capital items.
  - The benefits derived from such purchases are likely to be derived over several years.
- Capital investment appraisal is a technique whereby long-term capital projects may be considered:
  - to determine project viability,
  - to rank projects where there is a choice between alternatives.
- The principal methods used for capital investment appraisal are:
  - accounting rate of return (ARR),
  - payback method,
  - net present value (NPV),
  - internal rate of return (IRR).
- The decision rule for ARR is:
  - projects that generate a return in excess of the organisation's cost of capital may be selected;
  - where there is a choice between alternatives, the project with the highest ARR should be chosen.
- The decision rule for payback is:
  - to select the project with the shortest payback period.

- The decision rule for NPV is:
  - NPV must be positive for a project to be viable;
  - to select the project with the highest NPV.

- The decision rule for IRR is:
  - IRR must be above the cost of capital for a project to be viable;
  - to select the project with the highest IRR.

- Capital investment appraisal techniques do not take into account risk and uncertainty.
  - The use of sensitivity analysis and probabilities may prove useful in dealing with uncertainty.
  - The use of standard deviation may prove useful in dealing with risk.

Questions for review

1 Why is capital investment appraisal useful for long-term decision making?

2 Define ARR.

3 Describe how payback overcomes the limitations of ARR.

4 Explain the principle of compound interest and describe its relevance to discounted cash flow.

5 Define NPV and demonstrate how it may be calculated.

6 Explain the decision rule for NPV.

7 Define IRR and demonstrate how it may be calculated.

8 Explain the decision rule for IRR.

9 Explain the significance of the time value of money for NPV and IRR.

10 Explain how risk and uncertainty may be accommodated in the analysis for long-term decision making.

Self-assessment questions

(*Denotes that a suggested solution may be found at the end of this book.)

1* Accounting rate of return
Smith Brothers are considering the purchase of a new machine. There are two types available in the market, x and y. Details are as follows:

	Machine x (£)	Machine y (£)
Cost (Yr0)	(10,000)	(10,000)
Estimate residual value	2,000	3,000
Estimated life	4 years	4 years
Estimated future profits (before depreciation)		
Yr1	1,000	5,000
Yr2	5,000	3,000
Yr3	3,000	1,000
Yr4	5,000	2,000

Based upon the ARR, which machine would be purchased?

2* Payback

Jones Brothers are considering the purchase of a new machine. There are two types in the market, P and Q. Details are as follows:

	P (£)	Q (£)
Cost (Yr0)	(10,000)	(10,000)
Future cash inflows		
Yr1	2,000	5,000
Yr2	2,000	5,000
Yr3	6,000	1,000
Yr4	7,000	500
Yr5	8,000	500
	25,000	12,000

Based upon payback, which machine would be purchased? Comment on the decision taken in the light of the overall cash inflows generated by each machine.

3* Net present value

Company A is considering whether to invest £18,000 in a project, which would make cash profits as follows:

	£
Year 1	10,000
Year 2	8,000
Year 3	6,000

Cost of capital is 10%.

Calculate the NPV for the project and determine whether it is worth undertaking.

4* Internal rate of return

Company B is considering whether to invest £22,000 in a project, which would make cash profits as follows:

	£
Year 1	8,000
Year 2	10,000
Year 3	6,000
Year 4	4,000

Determine the IRR on the project.

5 Net present value vs. internal rate of return

Company C is considering whether to invest in Mutually Exclusive Projects (i.e. one cannot undertake both projects), which would make cash profits as follows:

Year	Project 1 (£)	Project 2 (£)
0	(20,000)	(2,000)
1	12,000	1,300
2	12,000	1,300

The cost of capital is 10%. Only one project can be undertaken.

a Calculate the NPV of each proposal.
b Calculate the IRR of each proposal.
c Discuss your findings.

Appendix A

Present value and annuity tables

PRESENT VALUE TABLE

Present value of 1 (where r = discount rate; n = number of periods until payment)

Periods (n)	1%	2%	3%	4%	5%	6%	7%	8%	9%	10%
1	0.990	0.980	0.971	0.962	0.952	0.943	0.935	0.926	0.917	0.909
2	0.980	0.961	0.943	0.925	0.907	0.890	0.873	0.857	0.842	0.826
3	0.971	0.942	0.915	0.889	0.864	0.840	0.816	0.794	0.772	0.751
4	0.961	0.924	0.888	0.855	0.823	0.792	0.783	0.735	0.708	0.683
5	0.951	0.906	0.863	0.822	0.784	0.747	0.713	0.681	0.650	0.621
6	0.942	0.888	0.837	0.790	0.746	0.705	0.666	0.630	0.596	0.564
7	0.933	0.871	0.813	0.760	0.711	0.665	0.623	0.583	0.547	0.513
8	0.923	0.853	0.789	0.731	0.677	0.627	0.582	0.540	0.502	0.467
9	0.914	0.837	0.766	0.703	0.645	0.592	0.544	0.500	0.460	0.424
10	0.905	0.820	0.744	0.676	0.614	0.558	0.508	0.463	0.422	0.386
11	0.896	0.804	0.722	0.650	0.585	0.527	0.475	0.429	0.388	0.350
12	0.887	0.788	0.701	0.625	0.557	0.497	0.444	0.397	0.356	0.319
13	0.879	0.773	0.681	0.601	0.530	0.469	0.415	0.368	0.326	0.290
14	0.870	0.758	0.661	0.577	0.505	0.442	0.388	0.340	0.299	0.263
15	0.861	0.743	0.642	0.555	0.481	0.417	0.362	0.315	0.275	0.239

	11%	12%	13%	14%	15%	16%	17%	18%	19%	20%
1	0.901	0.893	0.885	0.877	0.870	0.862	0.855	0.847	0.840	0.833
2	0.812	0.797	0.783	0.769	0.756	0.743	0.731	0.718	0.706	0.694
3	0.731	0.712	0.693	0.675	0.658	0.641	0.624	0.609	0.593	0.579
4	0.659	0.636	0.613	0.592	0.572	0.552	0.534	0.516	0.499	0.482
5	0.593	0.567	0.543	0.519	0.497	0.476	0.456	0.437	0.419	0.402
6	0.535	0.507	0.480	0.456	0.432	0.410	0.390	0.370	0.352	0.335
7	0.482	0.452	0.425	0.400	0.376	0.354	0.333	0.314	0.296	0.279
8	0.434	0.404	0.376	0.351	0.327	0.305	0.285	0.266	0.249	0.233
9	0.391	0.361	0.333	0.308	0.284	0.263	0.243	0.225	0.209	0.194
10	0.352	0.322	0.295	0.270	0.247	0.227	0.208	0.191	0.176	0.162
11	0.317	0.287	0.261	0.237	0.215	0.195	0.178	0.162	0.148	0.135
12	0.286	0.257	0.231	0.208	0.187	0.168	0.152	0.137	0.124	0.112
13	0.258	0.229	0.204	0.182	0.163	0.145	0.130	0.116	0.104	0.093
14	0.232	0.205	0.181	0.160	0.141	0.125	0.111	0.099	0.088	0.078
15	0.209	0.183	0.160	0.140	0.123	0.108	0.095	0.084	0.074	0.065

ANNUITY TABLE

Present value of an annuity of 1 (where r = interest rate; n = number of periods)

Periods (n)	\multicolumn{10}{c}{Discount rates (r)}
	1%	2%	3%	4%	5%	6%	7%	8%	9%	10%
1	0.990	0.980	0.971	0.962	0.952	0.943	0.935	0.926	0.917	0.909
2	1.970	1.942	1.913	1.886	1.859	1.833	1.808	1.783	1.759	1.736
3	2.941	2.884	2.829	2.775	2.723	2.673	2.624	2.577	2.531	2.487
4	3.902	3.808	3.717	3.630	3.546	3.465	3.387	3.312	3.240	3.170
5	4.853	4.713	4.580	4.452	4.329	4.212	4.100	3.993	3.890	3.791
6	5.795	5.601	5.417	5.242	5.076	4.917	4.767	4.623	4.486	4.355
7	6.728	6.472	6.230	6.002	5.786	5.582	5.389	5.206	5.033	4.868
8	7.652	7.325	7.020	6.733	6.463	6.210	5.971	5.747	5.535	5.335
9	8.566	8.162	7.786	7.435	7.108	6.802	6.515	6.247	5.995	5.759
10	9.471	8.983	8.530	8.111	7.722	7.360	7.024	6.710	6.418	6.145
11	10.37	9.787	9.253	8.760	8.306	7.887	7.499	7.139	6.805	6.495
12	11.26	10.58	9.954	9.385	8.863	8.384	7.943	7.536	7.161	6.814
13	12.13	11.35	10.63	9.986	9.394	8.853	8.358	7.904	7.487	7.103
14	13.00	12.11	11.30	10.56	9.899	9.295	8.745	8.244	7.786	7.367
15	13.87	12.85	11.94	11.12	10.38	9.712	9.108	8.559	8.061	7.606

	11%	12%	13%	14%	15%	16%	17%	18%	19%	20%
1	0.901	0.893	0.885	0.877	0.870	0.862	0.855	0.847	0.840	0.833
2	1.713	1.690	1.668	1.647	1.626	1.605	1.585	1.566	1.547	1.528
3	2.444	2.402	2.361	2.322	2.283	2.246	2.210	2.174	2.140	2.106
4	3.102	3.037	2.974	2.914	2.855	2.798	2.743	2.690	2.639	2.589
5	3.696	3.605	3.517	3.433	3.352	3.274	3.199	3.127	3.058	2.991
6	4.231	4.111	3.998	3.889	3.784	3.685	3.589	3.498	3.410	3.326
7	4.712	4.564	4.423	4.288	4.160	4.039	3.922	3.812	3.706	3.605
8	5.146	4.968	4.799	4.639	4.487	4.344	4.207	4.078	3.954	3.837
9	5.537	5.328	5.132	4.946	4.772	4.607	4.451	4.303	4.163	4.031
10	5.889	5.650	5.426	5.216	5.019	4.833	4.659	4.494	4.339	4.192
11	6.207	5.938	5.687	5.453	5.234	5.029	4.836	4.656	4.486	4.327
12	6.492	6.194	5.918	5.660	5.421	5.197	4.988	4.793	4.611	4.439
13	6.750	6.424	6.122	5.842	5.583	5.342	5.118	4.910	4.715	4.533
14	6.982	6.628	6.302	6.002	5.724	5.468	5.229	5.008	4.802	4.611
15	7.191	6.811	6.462	6.142	5.847	5.575	5.324	5.092	4.876	4.675

Appendix B

Solutions to self-assessment questions

Chapter 2

1 (a)

	£
Direct labour – factory wages	26,000
Direct materials – missiles	63,750
Prime cost:	89,750

(b)

	£
Prime cost (as (a) above)	89,750
Indirect labour cost – factory wages	14,000
Indirect material cost – other materials	7,500
Machinery costs – machine depreciation	29,000
Establishment costs:	
Rent and rates	8,880
Telephone and postage	2,250
Cost of production:	151,380

(c)

	£	£
Cost of production (as (b) above)		151,380
Sales and distribution costs:		
Rent and rates	1,560	
Cleaning materials	1,875	
Telephone and postage	12,750	
Office wages	9,000	
Salespeople's motor expenses	9,000	
Delivery costs	15,000	
Advertising costs	17,000	
		66,185
Administration costs:		
Cleaning materials	1,875	
Rent and rates	1,560	
Office wages	9,000	
		12,435
Total cost:		230,000

(d)

	£
Indirect labour cost – factory wages	14,000
Indirect material cost – other materials	7,500
Machinery costs – machine depreciation	29,000
Establishment costs:	
Rent and rates	8,880
Telephone and postage	2,250
Factory overhead:	61,630

(e)

	£
Factory overhead (as (d) above)	61,630
Sales and distribution costs (as (c) above)	66,185
Administration costs (as (c) above)	12,435
Total overhead:	140,250

2   (a) Direct material
(b) Direct material
(c) Indirect labour
(d) Administration costs
(e) Direct labour
(f) Direct materials
(g) Machinery costs
(h) Establishment costs
(i) Administration costs
(j) Sales and distribution costs
(k) Sales and distribution costs
(l) Sales and distribution costs
(m) Indirect wages
(n) Financial costs
(o) Sales and distribution costs and administration costs
(p) Sales and distribution costs and administration costs
(q) Indirect material costs
(r) Machinery costs
(s) Indirect labour costs
(t) Direct material

Chapter 3

1

(a)

	Transactions	Total cost
High	925	950
Low	650	675
Change	275	275

$$\text{Variable cost} = \frac{\text{Change in cost}}{\text{Change in output/activity}} = \frac{275}{275} = £1$$

The fixed cost element of the total cost may now also be determined.

At an output of 925 transactions where the cost is £950:

	£
Variable cost (925 × £1)	925
Total cost	950
Therefore, fixed cost	25

At an output of 700 transactions:

	£
Variable cost (700 × £1)	700
Fixed cost	25
	725

(b) Using the fixed and variable cost data in (a) above:

At an output of 850 transactions:

	£
Variable cost (850 × £1)	850
Fixed cost	25
	875

3 $y = a + b(x)$

$ = 500 + 15(x)$

At activity level of 100:

$y = 500 + 15(100)$

$ = 2000$

Therefore, Total cost = £2000

At activity level of 150:

$y = 500 + 15(150)$

$ = 2750$

Therefore, Total cost = £2750

At activity level of 200:

$y = 500 + 15(200)$

$ = 3500$

Therefore, Total cost = £3500

4 $y = a + b(x)$

$220 = a + b(20)$

$120 = a + b(10)$

$\overline{}$

$100 = b(10)$

$\dfrac{100}{10} = b$

Therefore, b (variable cost) = £10

Substituting b into equation above

$220 = a + 10(20)$

$220 = a + 200$

Therefore, a (fixed cost) $= £20$

Chapter 4

1

	£
Labour	330 ($£5.50 \times 12$ units $\times 5$ days)
Overhead	200
Total production cost for a week:	530

3

	£
Labour (basic rate)	210 ($£6 \times 35$ hrs)
Labour ($1.5 \times$ basic rate)	22.5 ($1.25 \times £6 \times 3$ hrs)
Labour ($2 \times$ basic rate)	24 ($2 \times £6 \times 2$ hrs)
Total labour cost for week 4:	256.5

Chapter 5

1

(a) Receipt/issue date	Quantity	Price (£)	Issue details (£)	Balance (£)
17/08	150	1.50		$150 \times 1.50 = £225$
18/08			$55 \times 1.50 = £82.50$	$95 \times 1.50 = £142.50$
19/08	120	1.75		$95 \times 1.50 = £142.50$
				$120 \times 1.75 = £210.00$
20/08			$70 \times 1.50 = £105$	$25 \times 1.50 = £37.50$
				$120 \times 1.75 = £210.00$
21/08	25	1.70		$25 \times 1.50 = £37.50$
				$120 \times 1.75 = £210.00$
				$25 \times 1.70 = £42.50$
22/08	12	1.45		$25 \times 1.50 = £37.50$
				$120 \times 1.75 = £210.00$
				$25 \times 1.70 = £42.50$
				$12 \times 1.45 = £17.40$
23/08	22	1.80		$25 \times 1.50 = £37.50$
				$120 \times 1.75 = £210.00$
				$25 \times 1.70 = £42.50$
				$12 \times 1.45 = £17.40$
				$22 \times 1.80 = £39.60$
24/08			$25 \times 1.50 = £37.50$	$70 \times 1.75 = £122.50$
			$50 \times 1.75 = £87.50$	$25 \times 1.70 = £42.50$
			$£125.00$	$12 \times 1.45 = £17.40$
				$22 \times 1.80 = £39.60$
31/08 Stock valuation				£222

(b)

Receipt/issue date	Quantity	Price (£)	Issue details (£)	Balance (£)
17/08	150	1.50		$150 \times 1.50 = £225$
18/08			$55 \times 1.50 = £82.50$	$95 \times 1.50 = £142.50$
19/08	120	1.75		$95 \times 1.50 = £142.50$
				$120 \times 1.75 = £210.00$
20/08			$70 \times 1.75 = £122.50$	$95 \times 1.50 = £142.50$
				$50 \times 1.75 = £87.50$
21/08	25	1.70		$95 \times 1.50 = £142.50$
				$50 \times 1.75 = £87.50$
				$25 \times 1.70 = £42.50$
22/08	12	1.45		$95 \times 1.50 = £142.50$
				$50 \times 1.75 = £87.50$
				$25 \times 1.70 = £42.50$
				$12 \times 1.45 = £17.40$
23/08	22	1.80		$95 \times 1.50 = £142.50$
				$50 \times 1.75 = £87.50$
				$25 \times 1.70 = £42.50$
				$12 \times 1.45 = £17.40$
				$22 \times 1.80 = £39.60$
24/08			$22 \times 1.80 = \quad £39.60$	$95 \times 1.50 = £142.50$
			$12 \times 1.45 = \quad £17.40$	$34 \times 1.75 = £59.50$
			$25 \times 1.70 = \quad £42.50$	
			$16 \times 1.75 = \quad \underline{£28.00}$	
			$£127.50$	
31/08 Stock valuation				£202

(c)

Receipt/issue date	Quantity	Price (£)	Issue details (£)	Balance (£)
17/08	150	1.50		$150 \times 1.50 = £225$
18/08			$55 \times 1.50 = £82.50$	$95 \times 1.50 = £142.50$
19/08	120	1.75		(W1)
				$215 \times 1.64 = £352.60$
20/08			$70 \times 1.64 = £114.80$	$145 \times 1.64 = £237.80$
21/08	25	1.70		(W2)
				$170 \times 1.65 = £280.50$
22/08	12	1.45		(W3)
				$182 \times 1.64 = £298.48$
23/08	22	1.80		(W4)
				$204 \times 1.66 = £338.64$
24/08			$75 \times 1.66 = £124.50$	$129 \times 1.66 = £214.14$
31/08 Stock valuation				£214.14

Workings
(W1)

		£
95	stock units × £1.50 =	142.50
120	stock units × £1.75 =	210.00
215		352.50

£352.50/215 units = £1.639 534 8 rounded to £1.64

(W2)

		£
145	stock units × £1.64 =	237.80
25	stock units × £1.70 =	42.50
170		280.30

£280.30/170 units = £1.648 823 5 rounded to £1.65

(W3)

		£
170	stock units × £1.65 =	280.50
12	stock units × £1.45 =	17.40
182		297.90

£297.90/182 units = £1.636 813 1 rounded to £1.64

(W4)

		£
182	stock units × £1.64 =	298.48
22	stock units × £1.80 =	39.60
204		338.08

£338.08/204 units = £1.657 254 rounded to £1.66

(d)

Receipt/issue date	Quantity	Price (£)	Issue details (£)	Balance (£)
17/08	150	1.50		150 × 1.65 = £247.50
18/08			55 × 1.65 = £90.75	95 × 1.65 = £156.75
19/08	120	1.75		215 × 1.65 = £354.75
20/08			70 × 1.65 = £115.50	145 × 1.65 = £239.25
21/08	25	1.70		170 × 1.65 = £280.50
22/08	12	1.45		182 × 1.65 = £300.30
23/08	22	1.80		204 × 1.65 = £336.60
24/08			75 × 1.65 = £123.75	129 × 1.65 = £212.85
31/08 Stock valuation				£212.85

(e) Receipt/issue date	Quantity	Price (£)	Issue details (£)	Balance (£)
17/08	150	1.50		$150 \times 1.50 = £225$
18/08			$55 \times 1.50 = £82.50$	$95 \times 1.50 = £142.50$
19/08	120	1.75		$215 \times 1.75 = £376.25$
20/08			$70 \times 1.70 = £119$	$145 \times 1.70 = £246.50$
21/08	25	1.70		$170 \times 1.70 = £289$
22/08	12	1.45		$182 \times 1.45 = £263.9$
23/08	22	1.80		$204 \times 1.80 = £367.20$
24/08			$75 \times 1.87 = £140.25$	$129 \times 1.87 = £241.23$
31/08 Stock valuation				£241.23

Chapter 6

1 (a) $\dfrac{£90,000 \text{ (overhead)}}{£4,000 \text{ (direct labour hours)}} = £22.50$ per direct labour hour

(b) $\dfrac{£90,000 \text{ (overhead)}}{£16,000 \text{ (machinery hours)}} = £5.625$ per machine hour

(c) $\dfrac{£90,000 \text{ (overhead)}}{£20,000 \text{ (direct labour cost)}} = £4.50$ per £1 of direct labour cost

(d) $\dfrac{£90,000 \text{ (overhead)}}{£45,000 \text{ (machinery cost)}} = £2$ per £1 of machinery cost

2

	£
Direct cost	12
Overhead	90 (4 hrs × £22.50)
Total cost	102

3 Overhead per fridge: 4 hrs × £22.50 = £90

$\dfrac{\text{Total overhead}}{\text{Overhead/unit}} = $ No. of units to recover overhead

Therefore, $\dfrac{£90,000}{£90} = 1,000$ fridges will need to be made and sold to recover all overheads

4 **(a)**

	M £	A £	F £	S £
Allocated overhead:				
Indirect materials	1,800	2,000	2,600	–
Indirect wages	1,200	1,000	2,400	3,000
Sub-total	3,000	3,000	5,000	3,000
Apportioned overhead:				
Rent (W1)	656.25	1,531.25	1,093.75	218.75
Rates (W1)	468.75	1,093.75	781.25	156.25
Light and Heat (W1)	871.87	2,034.37	1,453.12	290.62
Building repairs (W1)	1,031.25	2,406.25	1,718.75	343.75
Plant depreciation (W2)	2,080.00	1,040.00	2,080.00	–
Sub-total	5,108.12	8,105.62	7,126.87	1,009.37
Total overhead	8,108.12	11,105.62	12,126.87	4,009.37
Stores – apportioned (W3)	801.87	1,603.75	1,603.75	(4,009.37)
Total	8,909.99	12,709.37	13,730.62	NIL

Workings
(W1) Apportioned according to proportion of floor space occupied
(W2) Apportioned according to proportion of machine hours
(W3) Apportioned according to the number of stores requisitions

(i) Overhead absorption rate for cost centre M using a direct labour hours basis:
$$\frac{8,909.99}{3,000} = £2.96999 \text{ rounded to } £2.97$$

(ii) Overhead absorption rate for cost centre A using a machine hours basis:
$$\frac{12,709.37}{2,000} = £6.35468 \text{ rounded to } £6.35$$

(iii) Overhead absorption rate for cost centre F using a direct labour hours basis:
$$\frac{13,730.62}{1,750} = £7.84606 \text{ rounded to } £7.85$$

(b)

		£
Machining Dept	(2 hours × £2.97)	5.94
Assembly Dept	(2 hrs × £6.35)	12.70
Finishing Dept	(3 hrs × £7.85)	23.55
Total overhead burden for one unit of production:		42.19

(c)

	£
Direct costs	25.00
Overhead	42.19
Total product cost:	67.19

Chapter 7

Overhead	£	Cost driver	Budgeted volume	Rate
Machine activity	200,000	Machine hrs	(W1) 32,000 hrs	(W2) £6.25/hr
Production set-ups	20,000	Set-ups	(W3) 40 set-ups	(W4) £500/set-up
Engineering stores	40,000	Orders	(W5) 50 orders	(W6) £800/order

Workings

(W1) Product L: 4,000 units × 3 machine hrs/unit = 12,000 hrs
    Product H: 10,000 units × 2 machine hrs/unit = 20,000 hrs
    _____
    32,000 hrs

(W2) £200,000/32,000 hrs = £6.25/hr

(W3) Product L: 10 set-ups
    Product H: 30 set-ups
    _____
    40 set-ups

(W4) £20,000/40 set-ups = £500 per set-up

(W5) Product L: 25 orders
    Product H: 25 orders
    _____
    50 orders

(W6) £40,000/50 orders = £800 per order

Total cost for a unit of L:

	£
Labour cost	2
Direct material	3
Direct costs	5

	£
Machine activity	75,000 (4,000 units × 3hrs) × £6.25
Production set-up	5,000 (£500 × 10 set-ups)
Engineering stores	20,000 (£800 × 25 orders)
	100,000

Units produced	4,000
Therefore, overhead unit	£25

	£
Direct costs	5
Overhead	25
Total cost	30

Total cost for a unit of H:

	£
Direct cost	2
Direct material	4
Direct costs	6

	£	
Machine activity	125,000	(10,000 units × 2 hrs) × £6.25
Production set-up	15,000	(£500 × 30 set-ups)
Engineering stores	20,000	(£800 × 25 orders)
	160,000	

Units produced	10,000
Therefore, overhead/unit	£16

	£
Direct costs	6
Overhead	16
Total cost	22

3 The following points would be relevant:

- The nature of the competitive environment
- Indirect costs are material and may not be assigned directly
- A description of the type of overhead that may be incurred
- A description of the types of activities carried out by the company
- The organisation should offer a diverse range of services

Chapter 8

1 Breakeven point (units): $\dfrac{\text{Fixed costs}}{\text{Contribution per unit}}$

$$\frac{£25,000}{(£20 - £15)} = 5,000 \text{ units}$$

Breakeven point (revenue): $\dfrac{\text{Fixed costs}}{\text{C/s ratio}}$

$$\frac{£25,000}{5/20} = £100,000$$

Margin of safety:

8,000 − 5,000 = 3,000 units
or
3,000 units × £20 = £60,000

2 **(a)**

	£
Sales	8,000
less variable costs	(2,560)
Contribution	5,440
less fixed costs	(3,340)
Profit	2,100

(b)

	£
Sales	7,400
less variable costs	(2,368)
Contribution	5,032
less fixed costs	(3,340)
Profit	1,692

6 *Workings*

	£/unit	
Direct material	1.25	(£15,000/12,000 units)
Direct labour	1.00	(£12,000/12,000 units)
Variable expenses	0.50	(£6,000/12,000 units)
Total variable cost	2.75	
Fixed costs	1.00	(£12,000/12,000 units)
Full cost	3.75	

Period 1

	Absorption costing		Marginal costing	
	£'000s	£'000s	£'000s	£'000s
Sales		50		50
Opening stocks	nil		nil	
Production cost:				
Direct material	15		15	
Direct labour	12		12	
Variable expenses	6		6	
Fixed costs	12		–	
	45		33	
Closing stock	(7.5)[(1)]		(5.5)[(2)]	
Cost of sales		(37.5)		(27.5)
Contribution		–		22.5
Fixed costs		–		(12)
Profit		12.5		10.5

Period 2

	Absorption costing		Marginal costing	
	£'000s	£'000s	£'000s	£'000s
Sales		60		60
Opening stocks	7.5[1]		5.5[2]	
Production cost:				
Direct material	12.5		12.5	
Direct labour	10		10	
Variable expenses	5		5	
Fixed costs	12		–	
	39.5		27.5	
Closing stock	nil		nil	
Cost of sales		(47)		(33)
Contribution		–		27
Fixed costs		–		(12)
Profit		13		15

[1] 2,000 units × £3.75 (full cost)
[2] 2,000 units × £2.75 (variable cost)

7 (a) Breakeven point (units):

$$\frac{\text{Fixed costs}}{\text{Contribution per unit}}$$

$$\frac{£50,000}{(£5 - £4)} = 50,000 \text{ units}$$

Breakeven point (revenue):

$$\frac{\text{Fixed costs}}{\text{C/s ratio}}$$

$$\frac{£50,000}{1/5} = £250,000$$

(b) Margin of safety:

80,000 − 50,000 − 30,000 units

$$\frac{30,000 \text{ units}}{80,000 \text{ units}} = 37.5\%$$

(c) Breakeven chart:

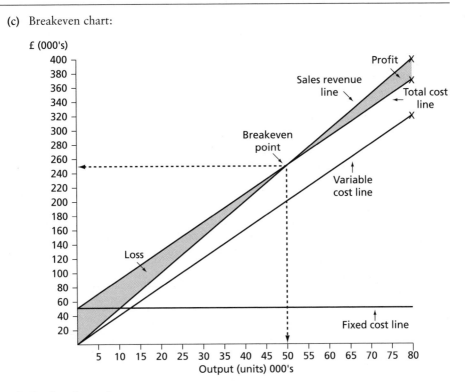

(d) Profit volume chart:

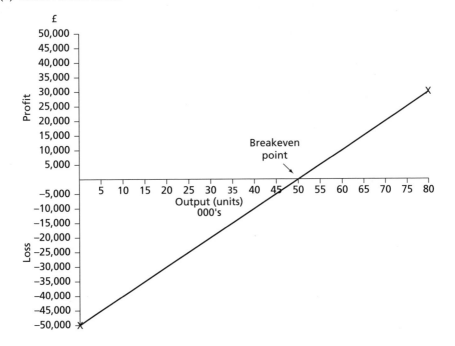

Chapter 9

1

	£/unit
Marginal cost of manufacture	15
Cost of buying in	18
Benefit of manufacture	3

The company should make, rather than buy the transistors.

2 (a) As the firm does have spare capacity and regular production would be unaffected, then the order could be accepted as the selling price of £8/unit is greater than the marginal cost of £7/unit. Fixed costs will remain unchanged as there is spare capacity. Additional contribution of (£8 − £7) × 2,500 units = £2,500 will be generated and overall profit will increase by the same amount.

(b) If the order were accepted, what would the reaction be of existing customers? Could the spare capacity be used for other more profitable work? Would the order, at a significantly lower price, lead to a change in pricing policy for all companies in the market?

3 (a)

Product	1	2	3	4
	£000's	£000's	£000's	£000's
Sales	550	750	200	260
Variable costs	330	600	100	360
Contribution	220	150	100	(100)

Products 1, 2 and 3 make a positive contribution and should be continued. Product 4 makes a negative contribution and should be discontinued.

(b) *Original production plan*

	£000's
Contribution: Product 1	220
Product 2	150
Product 3	100
Product 4	(100)
Total contribution	370
less fixed costs	(330)
Profit	40

Revised production plan as per recommendation in part (a)

	£000's
Contribution: Product 1	220
Product 2	150
Product 3	100
Product 4	nil (discontinued)
Total contribution	470
less fixed costs	(330)
Profit	140

If product 4 were discontinued, profit would be increased to £140,000. The increase in profit is the same as the negative contribution no longer incurred as a result of discontinuing product 4.

4 (a) All four products have a positive contribution. If there were no shortage of materials, the production plan would be the maximum demand for the products. However, given that material is in short supply contribution per kg of material (key factor or limiting factor) must be determined and the products ranked in order of preference for production.

Contribution per key factor:

Product	1	2	3	4
Contribution	8	10	9	5
Material/unit	2.5	5	1.5	2
Contribution per unit of material	3.2	2	6	2.5
Ranking	2	4	1	3

Production plan:

	kg
1,250 units of product 3 consuming	1,875
1,000 units of product 1 consuming	2,500
1,375 units of product 4 consuming	2,750
575 units of product 2 consuming	2,875
	10,000

Profit generated using contribution per key factor:

Product	1	2	3	4	Total
Production plan units	1,000	575	1,250	1,375	
	£	£	£	£	£
Contribution	8,000	5,750	11,250	6,875	31,875
Fixed costs					12,000
Profit					19,875

(b) *Production plan using ranking of contribution only (as opposed to contribution per key factor):*

Product	1	2	3	4	Total
Production plan units	150	1,550	1,250	0	
	£	£	£	£	
Contribution	1,200	15,500	11,250	0	27,950
Fixed costs					12,000
Profit					15,950

The profit generated using contribution per limiting factor (or key factor) is £19,875 − £15,950 = £3,925 higher than using ranking of contribution only.

177

Chapter 10

1 A rolling budget would be prepared in detail for (say) the first three months with less detail for the remainder of the year. At the end of each month (accounting period) a comparison is made between actual results and the original budget. Where conditions have changed on a permanent basis, the budget for the remaining months may be revised to reflect the new conditions anticipated. This approach assists planning and control as budgets are more realistic and achievable having been continuously updated. As each month is completed a further month's detail is added such that there is always a detailed budget available for the next three months.

2 (a) Budgeted output: 4,500 units
                            250 units
                          ─────────────
                          4,750 units

If 5% of the inspected units will be scrapped $4,750 \times 100/95 = 5,000$ units will have to be produced.

Labour budget: 5,000 units $\times$ £18 = £90,000
Material budget: 5,000 units $\times$ £10 = £50,000

(b) Scrap value of units: 250 units $\times$ £5 = £1,250

(*Note*: In certain circumstances, the scrap value of £1,250 could be deducted from the material budget of £50,000. The material budget would then be £48,750).

Chapter 11

2

	£	£
Actual materials @ actual cost	60	
(4 kg × 10 units × £1.50)		
Actual materials @ standard cost	56	(4) adverse price variance
(4 kg × 10 units × £1.40)	—	
Standard materials @ standard cost	42	(14) adverse usage variance
(3 kg × 10 units × £1.40)		

3

	£	£
Actual materials @ actual cost	250	
(actual materials cost for 420 cm)		
Actual material @ standard cost	210	(40) adverse price variance
(420 cm × £0.50)	—	
Standard material @ standard cost	250	40 favourable usage variance
(5 cm × 100 units × £0.50)		

4

	£	£
Actual materials @ actual cost (15,000 pieces total cost)	7,250	
Actual material @ standard cost (15,000 pieces at £0.56)	8,400	1,150 favourable price variance
Standard material @ standard cost (12 pieces × 1,000 tins × £0.56)	6,720	(1,680) adverse usage variance

Labour rate and efficiency variances	£	£
Actual labour hours @ actual rate (2,500 hours total cost)	8,000	
Actual labour hours @ standard rate (2,500 hours × £2.75)	6,875	(1,125) adverse rate variance
Standard labour hours @ standard rate (2 hours × 1,000 tins × £2.75)	5,500	1,375 adverse efficiency variance

To: The Board of Directors
The favourable material price variance indicates purchasing efficiency as material has been acquired cheaper than planned. However, more material has been used than planned, resulting in an adverse usage variance.

Both labour rate and efficiency variances are adverse, indicating that XY plc is paying more than planned for the labour, who in turn are not able to achieve the target (standard) time to produce a tin of output.

These variances may be related. It may be possible that purchasing efficiency was achieved by acquiring inferior, hence cheaper material, resulting in more material being scrapped, hence the usage variance, and longer labour times, hence the efficiency variance.

6 The variances are:
Material: price and usage
Labour: rate and efficiency
Variance overhead, expenditure and efficiency
Fixed overhead, expenditure and volume

Materials	£	£
Actual materials @ actual cost (25,000 metres × £0.21)	5,250	
Actual materials @ standard cost (25,000 metres @ £0.20)	5,000	(250) adverse price variance
Standard materials @ standard cost (25 metres × 1,100 units × £0.20)	5,500	500 favourable usage variance

Labour	£	£
Actual labour hours @ actual rate (1,200 hours × £4.95)	5,940	
Actual labour hours @ standard rate (1,200 hours × £4.75)	5,700	(240) adverse rate variance
Standard labour hours @ standard rate (1.2 hours × 1,100 × £4.75)	6,270	570 favourable efficiency variance

Variable overhead	£	£
Actual variable overhead	950	
Actual labour hours @ VOAR	1,800	850 favourable efficiency variance
(1,200 hours × £1.50)	———	
Standard labour hours @ VOAR	1,980	180 favourable efficiency variances
(1.2 hours × 1,100 units × £1.50)		

Fixed overhead	£	£
Actual fixed overhead	1,350	
Budgeted fixed overhead	1,500	150 favourable expenditure variance
(1.2 hours × 1,000 units × £1.25)	———	
Standard labour hours @ FOAR	1,650	150 favourable volume variance
(1.2 hours × 1,100 units × £1.25)		

Chapter 12

1

	Machine x £	Machine y £
Total profits	14,000	11,000
Asset life	4 yrs	4 yrs
Average profits	3,500	2,750
Value of investment at start	10,000	10,000
Value of investment at end	2,000	3,000
	12,000	13,000
Average investment (÷2)	6,000	6,500
ARR	$\frac{3,500}{6,000} = 58.33\%$	$\frac{2,750}{6,500} = 42.31\%$

Machine x would be chosen as it provides a better return of 58.33% compared with machine y with 42.31%.

2

	Machine P £	Machine Q £
Cost (yr 0)	10,000	10,000
Future cash inflows		
Yr1	2,000	5,000
Yr2	2,000	>5,000 < payback
Yr3	>6,000 < payback	1,000
Yr4	7,000	500
Yr5	8,000	500
	25,000	12,000

Machine Q should be chosen as the payback is at the end of year 2, whereas machine P pays back at the end of year 3. However, the returns from machine P are £13,000 greater than machine Q.

3

	£	10% discount factor	Present value £
Cost (Yr0)	(18,000)		(18,000)
Future cash inflows			
Yr1	10,000 ×	0.909 =	9,090
Yr2	8,000 ×	0.826 =	6,608
Yr3	6,000 ×	0.751 =	4,506
Net present value (NPV)			2,204

The forecast NPV is positive, therefore the project is worth undertaking.

4

	£	12% discount factor	Present value £	10% discount factor	Present value £
Cost Yr0	(22,000)		(22,000)		(22,000)
Yr1	8,000	0.893	7,144	0.909	7,272
Yr2	10,000	0.797	7,970	0.826	8,260
Yr3	6,000	0.712	4,272	0.751	4,506
Yr4	4,000	0.636	2,544	0.683	2,732
Net present value NPV			(70)		770

Using interpolation formula:

$$\text{IRR} = A + \left(\frac{a}{a+b} \times (B - A) \right)\%$$

$$= 10\% + \left(\frac{770}{770 + 70} \times (12 - 10) \right)\%$$

$$= 10\% + (0.9166 \times 2\%)$$

$$= 10\% + 1.83\%$$

$$\text{IRR} = 11.83\%$$

Index